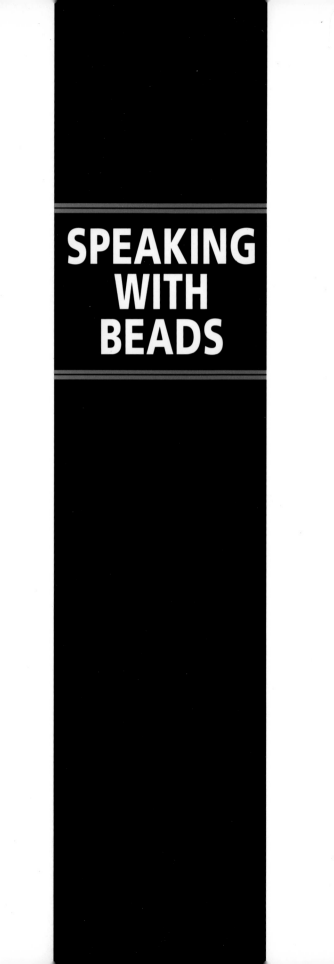

SPEAKING
WITH
BEADS

W9-ANP-160

SPEAKING WITH BEADS

Zulu Arts from Southern Africa

Jean Morris
Text by Eleanor Preston-Whyte

Thames and Hudson

Any copy of this book issued by the publisher
as a paperback is sold subject to the condition
that it shall not by way of trade or otherwise be
lent, resold, hired out or otherwise circulated
without the publisher's prior consent in any
form of binding or cover other than that in
which it is published and without a similar
condition including these words being
imposed on a subsequent purchaser.

© 1994 Jean Morris and Eleanor Preston-Whyte

First published in the United States of America
in 1994 by Thames and Hudson Inc.,
500 Fifth Avenue, New York, New York 10110

Library of Congress Catalog Card Number
94-60280

ISBN 0-500-27757-5

All Rights Reserved. No part of this publication
may be reproduced or transmitted in any form
or by any means, electronic or mechanical,
including photocopy, recording or any other
information storage and retrieval system,
without prior permission in writing from
the publisher.

Printed and bound in Singapore

CONTENTS

INTRODUCTION

In the mid-1970s Jean Morris, travelling in the country areas ofSouthern Africa, compiled a photographic record of the dress and decoration worn by rural African people. At that time she, along with many others, believed that the styles and way of life she encountered were destined to disappear in the face of Westernization and the encroachment of city life. Indeed, much has changed in recent decades but, as photographs taken in 1989 and 1991 when she revisited Natal and KwaZulu show, the use of beadwork is not one of them. While everyday life has seen the adoption of factory-made clothing and textiles, together with relatively cheap mass-produced costume jewelry, the finery and decoration chosen by many people for family celebrations, and that worn on public ceremonial occasions, has retained much of its local character, its novelty and, above all, its variety and individuality. It is in such activities that beadwork continues to play a major role in dress and in the expression of personal style.

More than this. There has been a conscious elaboration and fostering of local styles that include beaded decorations, and what many people believe to be 'traditional' dress, or elements of it, are worn with pride and are blended felicitously with the most sophisticated of modern dress. While completely new designs, often referred to by beadmakers as *isimodeni*, or

'modern', have appeared, older colour combinations and the distinctive patterns that identified regional beadwork styles have survived. Beadwork has also entered the international fashion world in the form of costume jewelry. Although beads and beadwork form the major theme of this essay, it is therefore from the changing context of their use in all forms of dress that they 'speak'.

On her return visits to Natal and KwaZulu Jean Morris met and collaborated with anthropologists Eleanor Preston-Whyte and Geraldine Morcom in compiling the interpretative text to accompany her photographs. Together they went to the annual religious pilgrimages of the thousands-strong Nazareth Baptist Church, while Jean Morris attended the celebration of the annual Reed ceremony at the royal capital of Nongoma. These events serve to illustrate the continuities and changes in the use of Zulu beadwork for both religious and ceremonial occasions. Because much of the earlier research done by Eleanor Preston-Whyte focused on the income-generating potential of Zulu craft for local women, the book also contains a chapter on making money through the 'updating' of beadwork skills to meet the growing tourist and art market for beautiful, as well as unusual, 'ethnic art'.

While it is beadwork in all its forms that provides the pivot of the discussion,

the authors have tried not to separate beadwork from the context in which it is worn – or in and for which it is made and designed. Accordingly they pay as much attention to bead workers and to the wearers of beads as to items of beadwork themselves. The title *Speaking with Beads* captures this intention for it is the communication, first between designer and wearer, and second, between wearer and audience, that is of interest to them.

Because Jean Morris's first and most extensive photographic trip to KwaZulu was made in the 1970s, many of the illustrations in the earlier chapters of the book come from this period. They record the styles of the time and particularly those of the Msinga and Muden areas. This region has long been famous for its beadwork and a fair amount of literature has recently become available to enrich the discussion both of the traditions and of the changes illustrated in the photographs. For those who wish to delve further into the intricacies of meaning, possible symbolism and the alternative interpretations of the styles of this and other regions, a full list of references is given at the end of the volume.

Who are the people who made and continue to make and wear the exquisite items illustrated in the pages of this volume? Zulu-speaking South Africans live in all the major urban centres of the country, to which they have been

Contemporary KwaZulu and Natal in relation to the location of the old Zulu Empire.

Cartographic Studio,Dept. of Geographical and Environmental Sciences,University of Natal,Durban,1994.

drawn in search of work and the benefits of modern life. Many, however, have homes and relatives in the rural areas of the region known officially as KwaZulu, but often referred to as 'Zululand'. This is situated on the eastern seaboard of South Africa (see map opposite) and although there are some small towns, most people are subsistence farmers eking out a living on small tracts of arable and grazing land. Most men and, recently, many women also, are, or have been, migrants living temporarily in cities such as Johannesburg and Durban. Education is by no means universal; some people, and particularly women living in remote areas such as Msinga, speak little English and some have only once or twice visited the towns where their husbands work. Their experience of the world beyond their homes comes largely from the radio and the tales of returning migrants. A decade or so ago only a minority of children went beyond the first few years at school and, in conservative homes, girls might not attend at all. Instead they were socialized to fill the roles expected of rural wives and mothers. In the face of poverty some women have found a market for beadwork skills, which girls learn as they begin to court and prepare for marriage.

Non-African South Africans feature in the book in that they buy and wear African beadwork. It was largely White and Indian business interests that provided the first conduits through which African beadwork reached the outside commercial market. This transformed it from a purely local craft, serving limited endogenous needs, to a money spinner in the international art and craft network. The heroines of the saga are, however, rural women who have used the skill of beadmaking to earn for themselves and their families the cash necessary to enter the modern world on an equal footing with other South Africans.

The book provides a combination of text and photographs so that it can be 'read' in different ways. Readers seeking a largely visual experience may focus on the photographs themselves, and on the striking and aesthetically exciting contrasts in form and colour that are thrown up within and between them. Alternatively, if the accompanying text is read along with the photographs, the appeal of the collection is an intellectual one which seeks to understand beads and beadwork in the context of contemporary life in Southern Africa, and particularly in relation to many of transformations through which the social order is moving. In this respect, *Speaking with Beads* is a book of the 1990s and, although rooted in photographs taken over the last two decades, the focus is on and from the present. In that it celebrates a vibrant and changing tradition, it speaks also of and to the future.

VOICES FROM THE PAST

'Nc'pae, a young Zulu in his dancing dress' by G.F. Angas (1849, plate xix).
The lithographs above left and right are based on watercolours executed during the artist's travels through the Zulu kingdom in the middle of the nineteenth century. Describing the dress of Nc'pae, Angus wrote: 'The dancing costume of young men was no less spectacular than was that of young women.'

Girl's coming-of-age girdle, *c.* 1890-1900. It is similar in design and colour to the beadwork depicted in the lithographs – from a slightly earlier period – reproduced opposite.

It is from their scarcity, as much as their beauty, that beads and beaded decorations derive their value and popularity in Southern Africa. Before the middle of the last century most beads were made locally of wood, shell, animal teeth or seeds and, in some areas, of clay. In addition, brass beads were highly prized because they were manufactured by smiths who were believed to have mystical powers. All beads were combined, particularly in the case of men's ceremonial dress, with feathers and animal skins and often with large bronze and copper arm rings. Because they were relatively rare, these decorations indicated power and achievement and, in the case of warriors, strings of metal beads were often the reward for feats of valour. In some areas locally made beads and other ornaments of dress might well have been augmented by the few foreign beads which filtered into Africa from early Arab trade. Eventually, however, imported glass beads became the most valued of all foreign goods.

Glass beads of European and especially Venetian manufacture first entered Southern Africa as trade goods imported largely through the East Coast port of Delagoa Bay. Established by the Portuguese as early as the sixteenth century, much of this trade was in slaves and ivory exchanged for all manner of foreign 'trinkets', including blankets and a variety of glass beads that were

'Two of king Panda's dancing girls' by G.F. Angas (1849, plate xix). Francis Fynn, another early traveller in Zululand, describes girls wearing not only glass beads, but also 'a double string of brass balls ... and brass bangles, the latter being worn round the arms'.[1]

Detail of the intricate design of a girl's girdle, *c.* 1890-1900, Greytown area. Examples in the Campbell Collection suggest some variety in both the colour and style of old beadwork, which may reflect local styles and colour preferences.

produced in European factories specifically for this purpose. In 1823 Henry Francis Fynn, one of the first Whites to travel extensively in Southern Africa, made an exploratory expedition to Delagoa Bay during which he observed the local trade in 'sea-cow and elephant ivory as well as ostrich feathers'.[2] He commented, however, that it was slaves who were the main objects of 'sale'. In time, trade in ivory superseded that in slaves.

By the end of the eighteenth century imported beads had reached what is now northern Natal, where the foundations of the Zulu empire were being forged by Dingiswayo, the uncle and protector of the young Shaka Zulu. By this time other European powers had joined the Portuguese in trading through Delagoa Bay and internal trade networks had been established by the indigenous people living between Delagoa Bay and northern Natal. Declaring trade in foreign goods to be his 'personal privilege', however, Dingiswayo ordered that any of his subjects engaging privately in the barter of foreign goods should be put to death. He thus established a royal monopoly over the distribution and use of imported beads, a practice which later kings were to continue. When he assumed power, the great Shaka himself decreed that all new bead varieties be brought to his capital and, if he and later kings so wished, only they and those whom they chose to honour were permitted to wear them.

In time a number of White traders, missionaries and – later – prospective settlers provided additional sources of

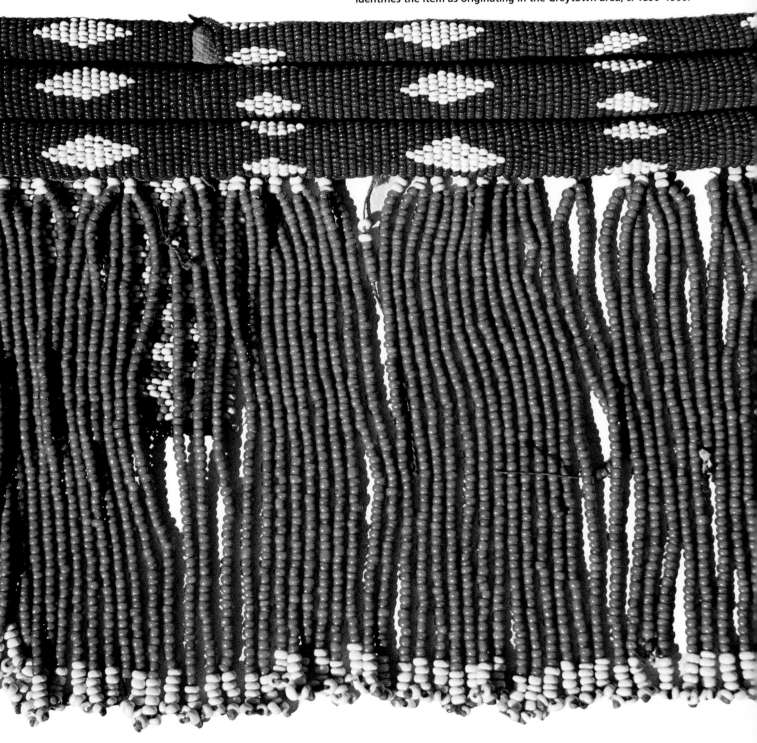

Detail of another girdle. The colour combination of blue next to white identifies the item as originating in the Greytown area, *c.* 1890-1900.

Three hip belts in different widths and designs. All c. 1890-1900, Greytown area.

glass beads to those imported through Delagoa Bay. Entering the region from the Cape, and later through Port Natal, many of these foreigners relied on beads to pay for food and service; they also sometimes used them to entice frightened or uninterested villagers to lend an ear to their message of a new religion. By the end of the nineteenth century some varieties of imported beads were so common that preferences for particular colours and sizes had developed. To the chagrin of travellers and traders, local people began to reject offers of beads not in keeping with regional styles.

It was not only through military superiority, but by the control of foreign goods, that the Zulu kings, together with their military leaders and court favourites, entrenched their position of privilege and power in the speedily growing nation and empire. Although based north of the Tugela river, Zulu hegemony stretched southwards to Port Natal. All foreigners entering the region were reported to the Zulu king and they brought with them gifts, including beads. Thus Fynn, arriving at Port Natal in 1824 to make preparations for the arrival of a contingent of British settlers, soon proceeded to the Zulu capital at the command of Shaka. Enlisting the company and advice of Francis Farewell, who had been trading in the country for some years, he presented the king with 'every description of beads at that time procurable in Cape Town, and far superior to those Shaka had previously obtained from the Portuguese at Delagoa'.[3]

The scene which greeted Fynn and Farewell at the court was spectacular, with the dancing of between 8,000 and 10,000 bead-clad maidens contributing in no small measure to its impact and grandeur. But . . . 'They had not been

Belt backed by canvas,
c. 1890 -1900.

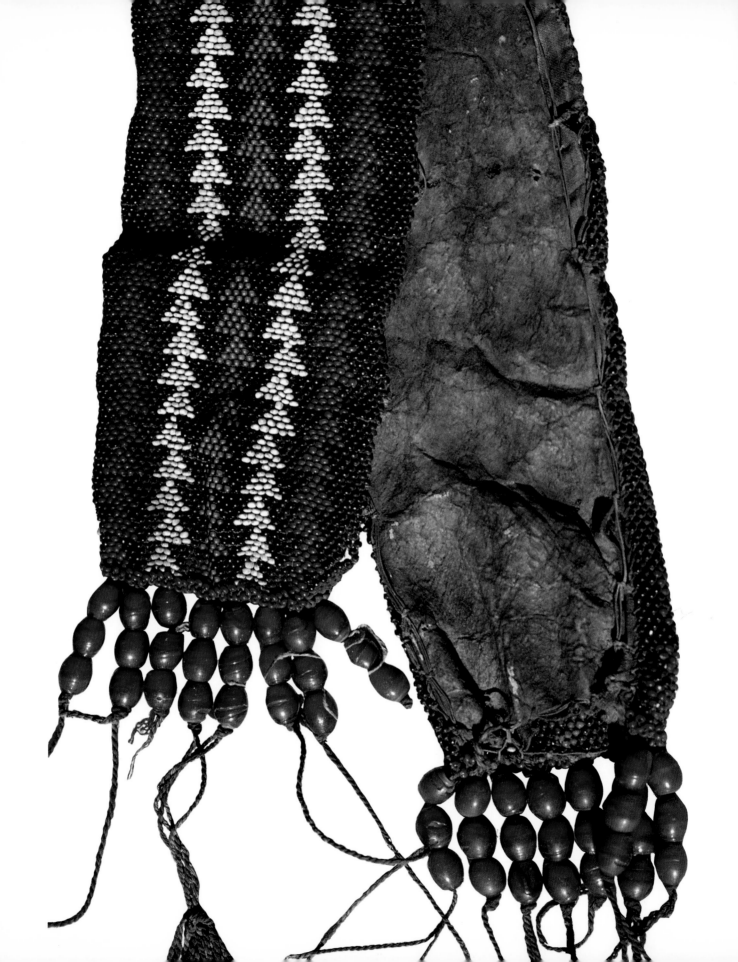

Opposite: **A leather-backed belt of a kind worn by married women after the birth of a baby, *c.* 1880 -1900. Large oval 'cornelian' beads are used to finish this and the belt on p.13. Deep red with white centres, cornelian beads were used extensively in trade in the late nineteenth century and help to date the items on which they were used. Another indication of the relative age of belts is their backing; earlier belts were built up on leather, but later ones incorporate canvas, cloth and, more recently, foam rubber.**

Early neck ornaments from Southern Natal. The beads are typically larger than those commonly used in Northern Zululand at the time.

From top to bottom: **Necklace, *c.* 1880; child's necklet, *c.* 1880 -1900; necklace, *c.* 1880.**

dancing many minutes, when they had to make way for the ladies of the Seraglio, besides about 150 others, who were called sisters. These danced in parties of eight, arranged in four, each party wearing different coloured beads, which were crossed from the shoulder to the knees. Each wore a head dress of black feathers, and four brass collars, fitting closely to the neck.'[4]

Fynn's observations of local life both before and after his first visit to King Shaka make it clear that by the middle of the last century imported beads had become deeply integrated into Zulu social life. Although no doubt admired for their beauty, they were far more than mere ornaments, for they had come to have cultural and symbolic meaning. The varieties and the colours of the beads that people wore (and were permitted to wear) immediately indicated their general social position, as well as any extraordinary personal achievements. Thus particular styles of beaded ornament characterized male as opposed to female dress and distinguished the young from the old, the married from the unmarried, commoners from royals and lords from their servants. Diviners and healers dressed differently from other people and were recognizable by their profuse use of beads even in everyday dress. Much of the beaded finery worn today operates in the same manner to highlight differences in marital status, gender, age and professional specialization.

It is important to emphasize that at the height of the Zulu Empire beads had considerable economic value. Their possession in large quantities was certainly a function of power and political influence but, because they were an important medium of exchange, it also distinguished the rich from the poor. Strings of beads were given in payment for goods and the services of smiths, doctors and diviners. There is oral evidence that, along with hoes, they preceded cattle as the original counters in marriage and bridewealth transactions. Beads also played an important part in the subsequent wedding ceremonies, for they adorned all who came to celebrate when the bride and her attendants danced for the first time in the midst of her new in-laws. Later they were used as the gifts that marked the symbolic integration of the bride into the family of her groom. They were used to cleanse mourners from the defilement of death, and when Shaka's mother Nandi died, the distraught king is said to have banned the wearing of beads for a year. Since beadwork played so pervasive a role in daily as well as ceremonial life, it is hardly surprising that it became intricate, complex and diversified into a highly developed art form which, as we will see in later chapters, included a distinct system of symbolic communication.

Although men as well as women incorporated beads into their dress, and especially into their dancing finery, it seems to have been women who wove the beads into necklaces and other jewelry. It may have been at the royal court, where large numbers of women served the kings either as wives or handmaidens and servants, that the earliest beadmaking skills and the first intricate designs developed. Later these skills would have spread throughout the kingdom as some of the royal women were released from court service, and either returned to their natal homes, or were given in marriage to important princes or commoners. It seems likely that these women would have taken with them at least some of the gifts and property they had acquired at court, including beads and the beaded ornaments amassed while serving the king. With the growing availability of beads they would also almost certainly have passed their skills in weaving beaded ornaments to their daughters and other women. Then, as now, it was probably young girls approaching marriage who were responsible for most beadwork, and for the development not only of distinctive regional styles, but also of the tradition of incorporating messages to their lovers and husbands in the gifts woven for them.

With the spread not only of White settlement, but of White entrepreneurship in Natal, beads became a regular feature of most commercial enterprises aimed at Black people. Traders in Europe provided beads to meet specific local demands, as a page from a typical catalogue shows (*opposite*). Eventually the ubiquitous trading stores in rural areas carried imported glass beads as part of their normal stock. Later plastic beads, which were manufactured in the country, joined them. Although cheaper and increasingly popular for some items, plastic beads have not displaced the popular glass variety completely. In particular, they have not gained much ground where the predominant market is a White or tourist one.

Beads are mentioned regularly in the diaries and journals kept not only by Fynn but also by missionaries and by many of the other early travellers, who visited the Zulu court and countryside. They appear also in drawings of the clothing worn by both royalty and commoners of the time. The Rev. Francis Owen, who lived for some time at uGungunlovu, the capital of Shaka's successor, King Dingaan, describes how the roof of the King's house was 'supported by 21 pillars or posts which are covered from top to bottom with beads of various colours.'[5]

Owen witnessed much the same massed dancing by beaded royal women as did Fynn in the time of Shaka. He describes it as follows: 'All his female servants who live at the back of the Isikauthlo [women's quarters], amounting in number to at least 500 and ornamented with beads, had been on occasion of my arrival summoned forth to sing . . . But the grand display was reserved for the last, when the King's women, 90 or 100 in number,

Page from a bead catalogue provided for potential traders by bead manufacturers in Europe, *c.* 1890-1920.

NATAL

SMALL ROUND BASUTO BEADS Size 0		LARGE ROUND BASUTO BEADS Size 2		MACANDA BEABS	
Green 943		White 4739		Yellow W	
Green 1270		Pink 891		Sky T	
Green 8		Royal 682		Ruby 767	
Yellow 784		Yellow 883		Crystal L	
Yellow 883		Blue 736		Chrome Or	
Yellow 18		Green 943		Blac	
Chrome 810		Black 871		Green Glass E	
Chrome 1005		White 937		Turquoise NT	
Blue 652		**LARGE ROUND BASUTO BEADS Size 3**		Amber H	
Blue 736		Yellow 1122		Chrome S.L.	
Blue 683		Saxe 730		Yellow W.C.	
Blue 4		Sky 948		White	
Blue 902		Royal 903		Coral Z.	
Blue 649		Black 871		**SMALL OVAL BEADS**	
1003		Red 112		Sky	
Royal 682		Red 1256		Royal	
Red 20104		Pink 891		Black	
Red 1561		Choc 907		Yellow	
Red 34		**MEDIUM OVAL BEADS**		Red	
Pink 891		Black		**SPECIAL CUT GLASS BEADS Size 10**	
Pink 563		Royal		Light Amber 047	
Pink 16		Sky		Ruby 879	
Pearl 606		Red		Royal 05	
Char 604		Yellow		**SPECIAL CUT GLASS BEADS**	
White 1		**CUT GLASS BEADS Size 12**		Ruby 879	
Black 12		Crystal 20024		Light Amber 047	

FLUTED BEADS

Black	
Red	
Yellow	

VICTORIAN BEADS

Sky	
Red	
Yellow	
Chocolate	
Black	
Royal	

advanced richly attired with beads and brass rings, which covered the greater part of their body.'[6]

He later describes the interest which the king took in the drawings of him in a copy of Gardiner's journal, *Narrative of a Journey to the Zoolu country*, which was sent to Owen at Dingaan's court. The king drew attention to 'the beads and various ornaments in which Capt. Gardiner had depicted him'.[7] In order to show the resemblance to the originals, Dingaan had a woman of his entourage don these items and pose with the pole depicted in the drawing.

Although not entirely clear, Gardiner's picture shows beaded garments and decorations very similar to those worn by men today as decoration on ceremonial occasions. Of interest also are the similarities which seem to exist between the beaded garments worn by Dingaan and examples of old beadwork in museum collections.

Even more evocative of the use of beadwork in ceremonial dress at the Zulu court are a series of lithographs made from watercolours executed by George French Angas, who visited Natal and Zululand in the middle of the

Beadwork dating from the end of the nineteenth century, reminiscent of that worn by King Dingaan in the Gardiner portrait above.

From top to bottom: Girl's girdle, *c.* 1890 -1910; girl's girdle, *c.* 1890 -1910; detail of a hip belt, *c.* 1890 -1900; detail of a married woman's belt, *c.* 1880 -1900.

Left: **King Dingaan as depicted by Captain Gardiner in his travelogue *Narrative of a Journey to the Zoolu country*.**

'Utimuni, Nephew of Shaka', by G.F. Angas (1849, plate xiii). 'The chiefs and principal people wear a profusion of beads, with heavy brass bangles from the wrist to the elbow' – Henry Francis Fynn

nineteenth century. Although many of the details may be romanticized, these pictures illustrate the general manner in which beads and beadwork added to the overall effect of dress. In one of them (see p. 9), two court maidens pose in costumes made almost entirely of beads. Angas's notation informs us that: 'On grand occasions the amount of beads worn by the King's women is almost incredible, a single dress having been known to consist of fifty pounds weight of these highly-valued decorations, so as to render it a matter of some difficulty as well as personal inconvenience for the wearer to dance under the accumulated weight of her beads.' The striking white, red and blue beads and the style of the beaded ornaments worn by both the young women and young man pictured on p. 9 are reminiscent of the elaborate and beautiful pieces of beadwork which date from the end of the last century (pp. 8, 18). How beadwork was combined with other elements of decoration is demonstrated admirably in Angas's depiction of Utimuni, the nephew of Shaka, with which this chapter ends (*right*). Angas noted of the young warrior that 'his kilts are of the finest skins; on his head are two globular tufts of the brilliant feathers of the blue and green roller; behind them is another, of eagles' plumes, with a snuff spoon stuck into the ring that surmounts his hair.'[8]

2
SPEAKING WITH BEADS

We move now from the past to the present. We will find, however, that there are continuities with the past as well as significant transformations in the use and functions of beadwork in contemporary Zulu life. The first and most dramatic change is that beadmaking and the wearing of beads is not characteristic of all or even most rural communities, and is certainly not a feature of everyday life in urban areas. In the countryside the split between families and communities which wear beads, and those that do not, is based on religion; where Christianity is the dominant form of worship, beadwork has all but died out. The reason for this is historical: early missionaries associated beadwork with heathen worship and converts were encouraged to lay them aside when, as part of their new life, they adopted the smocks and trousers that went with, and 'spoke' of, Church membership.

In this chapter we focus on the everyday life of people living in conservative rural areas where the ancestors are the centre of religious belief and where, in keeping with this, the organizational structures of domestic and neighborhood life may be described as 'traditional'. Although the photographs span the last twenty years, it is clear from those taken most recently that the style of dress has altered little: if anything, there has been an elaboration of beaded ornaments

A young married woman from Msinga, 1975. The belt is in the *isithembu* style, characterized by the panel of bright yellow beads. The belts are constructed on a base of woven grass onto which the beads and metal studs are sewn.

A young woman from the Msinga area, 1975. The coils on her headdress are typical of this region, and are made by lengthening her own hair with horsehair, firmly binding it into a coil and then decorating it with beads and studs. Some of her necklaces are in the *imvalimvali* style. They are built up from grass that is tightly bound with cotton to form a coil around which beads are wound.

A young man from Msinga with a beaded coil in his hair, 1975. His armbands are called *amaqulu*. Young men, like women, wear brightly coloured clothes to catch the eye, especially when courting. His belts are typical of the region (see also p. 42).

A woman wearing a cloak called *isibheklane*, an item of clothing unique to the lower Drakensberg area, 1975.

Two guests arrive at a wedding in the Umbumbulu area in 1976. The bead decorations on their cotton skirts are made separately and are either sewn or pinned onto the skirt fabric.

worn on special occasions, and beadmakers themselves speak of styles which are new, or *isimodeni*, and which have become popular only in the last generation.

The effects of missionary activity are epitomized in the distinction made in most Black South African rural areas between 'school' people, that is the descendants of Christian converts who attended school and who embraced Western culture, and those conservatives who rejected the new faith and often the schooling which, on mission stations, went with conversion. Various names are applied to these conservatives in different parts of the country but in Natal they are often referred to as *Amabinca* to distinguish them from 'school' people. As the illustrations in this chapter indicate, beadwork is only one element in *Amabinca* dress. It is combined with distinctive garments made of, for instance, locally cured cowhide, as well as modern materials like coloured cloths, sand shoes and plastic baubles bought from trading stores. The overall effect is very different to that of Western dress.

An unmarried girl wearing large panels of contemporary beadwork, on her way to a Saturday afternoon dancing party. Shongweni, 1975.

It is not only form but meaning that is important, and much as in the days when Henry Francis Fynn visited Zululand in the last century, dress indicates the general social position of the wearer. The sets of photographs on the following pages provide a convenient background for a short discussion of some of the more important ways in which dress and beadwork 'speak' not only of religion and world view, but also of gender, age and marital status.

Some of the photographs in this chapter were taken as people went about their everyday lives: going, for instance, to the store, paying a visit to neighbours or waiting for a bus. Nevertheless, the majority were taken on those important occasions for which people usually dress up, and for which they bring out their finery. Thus beaded ornaments invariably complement the costumes worn at weddings and the other ceremonies which, like the coming of age of a young girl, mark the stages in the lifecycle of most individuals. They are also characteristic of the dancing outfits adopted by young people who belong to both formal and informal rural youth organizations. It is usually in these uniforms that groups of girls and boys from different geographical areas perform at public events, and the distinctive colour and style of each uniform is matched in the beadwork that accompanies it. Because these are the occasions when youngsters often

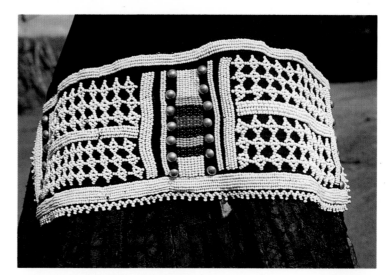

Opposite: A masterpiece of beadwork. This beaded cape with long bead tassels was worn proudly by a young woman from the Estcourt area in the lower Drakensberg in 1975.

Detail of beadwork on an apron worn by married women in the Weenen area, c. 1920-30.

Broad patterns of contemporary beadwork decorate the lower edge of black cotton aprons worn over cowhide skirts. The use of light green suggests the beadwork could be in the *umzansi* style. Melmoth area, 1975.

begin the courting that will lead to love affairs and eventually marriage, it is hardly surprising that each group strives to outdo the others in the beauty and spectacle of their attire.

The most distinctive features of the dress of mature women are the ornate headdress and the cowhide skirts which reach below their knees (pp.28-9). These indicate the married state of the wearer and, even when covered with a scarf, or nearly hidden by a colourful winding cloth, they produce a silhouette and gait that is unmistakable. In contrast, unmarried women and girls of marriageable age generally wear skirts which touch the knees, while very young girls often show most of their legs below tightly bound cloths. It is expected that the breasts of young unmarried girls will be uncovered and, particularly when girls are dancing, firm bosoms and tight thighs are much admired and taken as a positive indication of virginity and moral rectitude. In contrast, married women and sometimes girls who are about to wed, cover their breasts, shoulders and legs out of deference to their husbands and the families into which they have married or will marry. Of particular importance is the ubiquitous scarf or cloak adopted by married women out of respect for their husband's father and other senior men of the family.

Detail of a hip-belt worn by married women in the Valley of a Thousand Hills, Ndwedwe, c.1983.

Given the basic outline of what is appropriate dress, women and girls are free to give reign to their imaginations in decorating their costumes. Since beadmaking is their preserve, and skill in the art is much admired, they lavish on their costumes both creativity and minute attention to detail. Even the smallest ornament is made and placed with calculation. In this, beaded costumes speak of the wearer's personality as much as they do of her social status. Beadwork is also a way of communicating with lovers and husbands who are away in town, and some young women spend almost as much time creating beaded ornaments for men as they do for themselves. Girls may weave them for their brothers, but their role is usually to deliver the gifts of age mates to the men upon whom these girls have set their hearts.

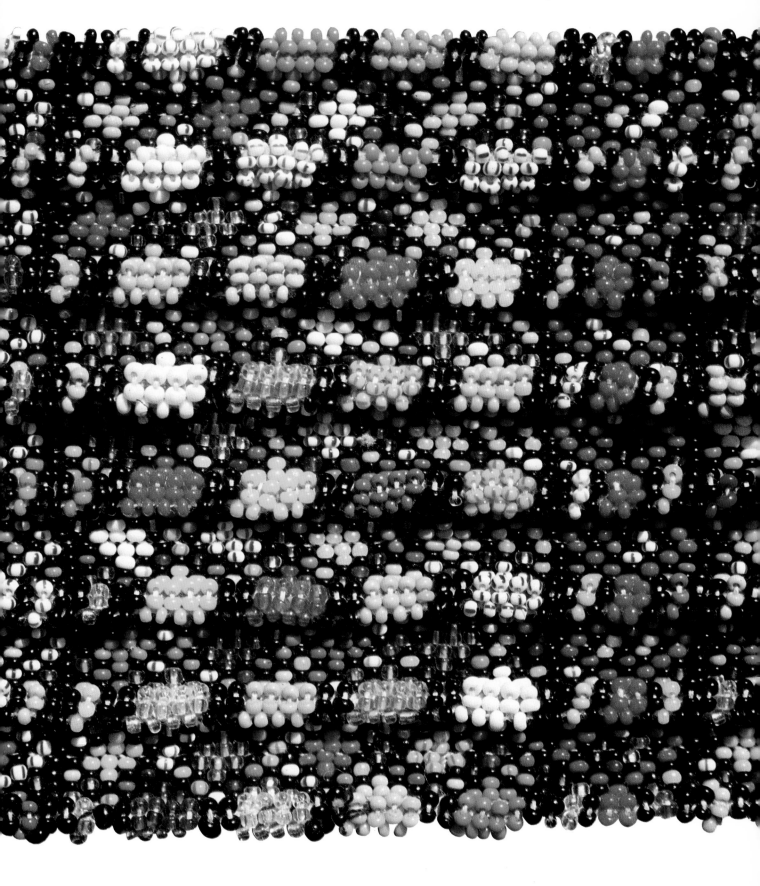

Above left: Beadwork decorates the back of a woman's head at Keat's Drift in the Msinga area, 1975. The headband in the *isinyolovane* pattern resembles Greytown beadwork, but the colour combination is that of Msinga.

Above right: A Msinga woman on her way to a wedding wearing a typical headdress of the area decorated in the *isithembu* style, 1974. Bead decorations are pinned to the headdress.

Left: A woman with a headband and decorated collar in the *umzansi* style, 1975. The headdress style shows that this woman is unmarried.

A young married woman in the Valley of a Thousand Hills wearing a richly beaded headdress which signifies her marital status. Her legs are covered with fine strings of white beads. 1979.

Below: Detail of the headdress. The shield motif is said to symbolize protection and security from attack.

A cap or *ikapisi* worn by an engaged youth from the Ladysmith area, *c.* 1940. Matching waistcoat worn for dancing, Estcourt area, *c.* 1950.

Dress conventions apply to men as well as women, although it is largely in their ceremonial and dancing dress that social and status distinctions are evident and beadwork most prominent. For most of the time, and certainly while they are at work, men and boys usually wear trousers, shirts and vests and it is only a beaded necklace, protruding briefly from the neck of a shirt, that speaks of the conservative world view of the wearer. Perhaps for this reason the impact of the costumes that men adopt for ceremonial occasions is all the more spectacular. They consist of skins, feathers and beads and, for dancing, are accompanied by a cowhide shield and assagai. A headring of animal skin often completes the outfit of men of authority, while princes of the blood are indicated by the inclusion of symbols of royalty in their dress. In the case of a young man, there is no reason not to sport, along with the necklaces given to him by his girlfriend, a colourful plastic pendant which might have caught his fancy at the local store. There is, of course, no reason why a young girl in the same area may not wear a similar bauble – as is illustrated by the photographs on page 21.

The waistcoat (*left*) was donned for dancing by a youth who explained the pattern on the left as *isilomi*, on the right as *isishunka* (see p.44), while the two crosses on the pockets are referred to as *isiambolosi*, or ambulance.

Man wearing the ceremonial headdress of a Zulu warrior reminiscent of the time of Shaka. He wears a profusion of beads and cross bands of beadwork over his shoulders. 1970s.

Guests at a royal wedding at Umbumbulu on the Natal South Coast in 1976. The patterns on the cross bands worn over the shoulder suggest that the wearer comes from Nongoma. Only men and unmarried women wear crossed shoulder belts.

Detail of the beadwork girdle shown above.

Girdle of a kind worn regularly by young unmarried girls from the Nongoma area. Men will, on special occasions, wear a similar girdle, but – unlike unmarried girls – men wear them on the hip.

Beadwork girdle worn by a married woman over her leather skirt or *isidwaba*, Ceza area, *c.* 1940.

A baby girl in the Muden area, 1975. African babies wear beads before clothes.

As they grow older, girls wear more and more beadwork. 1974.

Unless dressed for special occasions, children normally wear little beyond a shirt or old jersey when it is cold. Much of their time is spent on the back of their mother, grandmother or an elder sister where they are swathed in blankets. Small beaded waistbands and genital covers are woven for them and their ankles, wrists and necks are generally decorated with strings of beads by indulgent female relatives. As they grow older, pre-adolescent boys and girls may be distinguished by the increasing number of bead ornaments they begin to wear, culminating in the intricate and elaborate finery of their dancing costumes. These distinguish adolescents of different ages into a system of ordered age groupings, each of which has its leader and operates under the control of the age group immediately older than themselves. Such groupings are often referred to in a military idiom as regiments and those composed of young women match those for young men. Close ties are forged between age mates, but in the case of girls and women, these are often shortlived. Following strict rules of exogamy, they marry outside their kinship circle and this often entails

A young unmarried woman in the Valley of a
Thousand Hills. The headband is in the relatively
new *isimodeni* ('modern') style, 1970s.

Examples of modern plastic beadwork from the Ndwedwe area in the Valley of a Thousand Hills.

Small apron featuring large plastic beads made by Celani Ngubane, *c.* 1990.

Detail of part of a typical plastic bead belt, *c.* 1980-90.

Detail of a finely beaded panel using glass beads, Inanda area, Valley of a Thousand Hills, *c.* 1980.

leaving their natal area. For them both the membership of age groups and the beadmaking to which so much time is given in youth, is but a prelude to marriage, which in its turn has its appropriate beaded accoutrements and is ushered in with public dancing at which the bride often appears with her face hidden from sight by a beaded fringe. Later her first pregnancy is marked by a specially beaded apron (p. 40) while, for those who become diviners, a whole new style of dress is indicated in which beads vie with the inflated bladders of sacrificial animals for pride of place (p. 41).

Major events in the lives of young people and their families are the ceremonies held to celebrate marriage and, in the case of young women, to mark the fact that they have reached marriageable age. Referred to as *umemulo* or 'coming out', the latter is a public and joyous celebration of the potential fertility of a girl at which she dons, for the first time, the cowhide skirt of a married woman. With her age-mates and groups of older and younger women and girls, she dances in public and, as a symbol of the cattle her marriage will bring to the homestead, in the cattle byre of her father. The girl herself is richly dressed and her hair is decorated with 'paper money' by her family and well-wishers. Her shoulders and breasts are covered with the skin of a beast slaughtered to inform the ancestors that she has

Weddings and coming-of-age ceremonies are important events in the life of all communities. Here girls of different ages are distinguished by their dress as they wait for the dancing to begin during a ceremony at Muden, 1975.

Right: **Lines of girls join the dancing.**

Above right: **Bride's attendant.**

Far right: **The 'bride', an initiate diviner, has, in addition to her beadwork, a row of toffees sewn onto her headband for decoration. Note the typical Msinga beadwork colours – white, blue, red and green. The sticks are decorated in the** *isithembu* **beadwork style. Her future husband dances next to her. As the afternoon progresses, the tempo of dancing increases around the girl and her attendants.**

reached the age of marriage, after which she dances amid her peers for what is symbolically the last time before she leaves them in marriage.

The occasion is a serious one as well as one of joy. In their turn groups of younger girls in their short skirts, and older women in the full dress of their married station, entertain the assembled guests with massed dancing. They are followed by regiments of young men whose dancing is punctuated by virtuoso performances by individual dancers. The senior generation give the event their patronage and after the girl has danced in the cattle byre, they, too, dance and call out the praises of the family to which she belongs and those of her ancestors.

A male diviner photographed in the Hammersdale area of the Natal midlands, 1975. Diviners are recognizable by their long headdresses of white beads often topped by inflated bladders of the animals sacrificed to the ancestors, from whom they derive their 'sight' and power.

Right: A woman diviner with large plastic beads in her hair, Durban 1972.

Left: A married woman from the Tugela Ferry area near Msinga. She wears a richly decorated pregnancy apron made of the hide of an animal sacrificed to her husband's ancestors for the protection of the unborn baby. The apron is also believed to bring good luck and health to the child. 1975.

Izangoma, or diviners, are called by their ancestors to their profession, and they are apprenticed to a teacher for a number of years before beginning to practise on their own. During this time they are taught to contact the spirits for the inspiration that allows them to diagnose the causes of illness and misfortune, discover the location of lost or stolen objects, and, in some cases, to throw the bones in order to tell the future. In the old days diviners were the protectors of society and the confidants of princes. Today they are consulted when people are sick or beset by a run of bad luck and they are revered and sometimes feared for the sight that their ancestors are believed to give them.

In Natal women seem to outnumber men in the profession, although the men who do become diviners adopt the typical beaded costume with its flowing wig of white beads, crossed breast bands of skin, and beaded necklaces, anklets and wristbands. When they are dressed for ceremonial dances, or even when they are going about their everyday trade, this costume marks them off from ordinary people and speaks eloquently of their supernatural powers. It is the association with the ancestors who are the source of this power that is symbolized by the beaded fly whisk which they carry, and by the dried gall bladders which adorn their headdresses.

3
SPEAKING OF MEANING

A young woman from Tugela Ferry in the Msinga area. She wears rope necklaces and bead decorations in the *umzansi* style, 1975.

It is apparent from a cursory glance at many of the photographs in this volume that regularities occur in the manner in which beads of different types, colours and sizes are distributed over the surface of the items of which they form an integral part. The way in which beads have been combined with other decorative features, such as brass studs, buttons and, in some ceremonies, even brightly wrapped sweets, is also striking. Taken together, many of these features constitute distinctive and widely recognized styles. Although some of these point to personal characteristics, including marital status, the call to be a diviner, or, as we will see in Chapter 4, religious affiliation, both colour and pattern often have an additional regional referent. For those with experience in these matters, beadwork from particular geographical areas is immediately recognizable and, on the occasions when people from different places come together to dance, it is often by beadwork style that they are identified. Since many of Jean Morris's early photographs were taken in the Msinga and Muden areas, it is these styles that tend to predominate in this volume. We have, however, included examples of beadwork from other areas and particularly from the Royal capital of Nongoma for comparison.

Regional styles speak largely to the outsider. What of the meanings that colour and design may convey to the

Huge ear discs of cork or wood, popular in Msinga. The ears have been pierced and the earlobes have been gradually stretched since childhood. 1975.

A belt in the *umzansi* style with four colours, made in the Msinga area, 1975.

Detail of male sash or shoulder belt. The colour combination and sequence (green-red, green-black) suggests that this item might have originated in Nongoma, *c.* 1960.

Right: Necklet typical of Msinga area in the *isithembu* style, *c.* 1970-80s. Note the distinctive five-colour sequence and use of studs.

recipients of beaded ornaments, and to the audience for which costumes are designed and chosen? Zulu beadwork has long been thought to constitute a system of non-verbal communication, and much of its appeal has derived from the mystery thought to be associated with 'the language of beads'. We will explore something of this meaning in the pages that follow.

In discussing Msinga beadwork we are fortunate in being able to draw on the expertise of a number of local beadmakers who recently discussed their art with Frank Jolles.[9] They drew a clear distinction between old and modern beadwork styles. The former, dating from before 1960, is characterized by the use of linear bands of plain colour rather than a proliferation of designs. These made use of a restricted range of somewhat sombre colours in an ordered sequence. Four colour schemes made up this old style:

isishunka seven colours – white, light blue, dark green, pale yellow, pink, red and black.

isithembu five colours – light blue, grass green, bright yellow, red and black.

umzansi four colours – white, dark blue, grass green and red.

isinyolovane combination of any colours not consistent with the other schemes.

While not all colours have to be present, the scheme is identified by the absence of intrusive elements from other colour schemes. The term *isishunka* is said to have no specific meaning, although the names of the second and third schemes are those of clans or clan areas, while *isinyolovane* has complex connotations of perfection, charm and an excellent combination – describing well the mixture of colours it represents.

In many pieces of beadwork the plain bands of colour are enlivened by the use of studs (*above*) and, in the case of the multistranded collar on p. 48, small locks. It is in these elaborations, as much as in the manipulation of the colour sequences, that the originality of the maker is allowed to surface. After the 1960s it seems that individuality and 'fashion' began to influence production and, although the same basic colours remain dominant in much of the beadwork, new colours and in particular the use of small designs became fashionable. The *umzanzi* scheme proved adaptable, with black sometimes replacing the typical blue and bright new colours, such as orange, taking the place of the normal red. It was, however, the potentially open nature of *isinyolovane* that allowed for the most innovation. Along with colour variation there was a startling proliferation of geometric designs at this time. Eventually a new style, *isilomi* or *isimodeni* (modern), took over, with the net result that Msinga beadwork was utterly transformed. Fashion (*imfesheni*) is now the keynote and a new fashion sweeps the area every few years.

Below: A panel of beadwork sewn onto the
lower edge of a black cotton apron, worn by
married women from the Muden area, *c.* 1950.

Right: A necklace or *ngqi* and (below) an *isigege*
or apron. Both are in the *isishunka* style from
the Msinga area.

Below right: An *isipinifa*, or panel of beadwork,
on the lower edge of a black cotton apron,
Estcourt area, *c.* 1950.

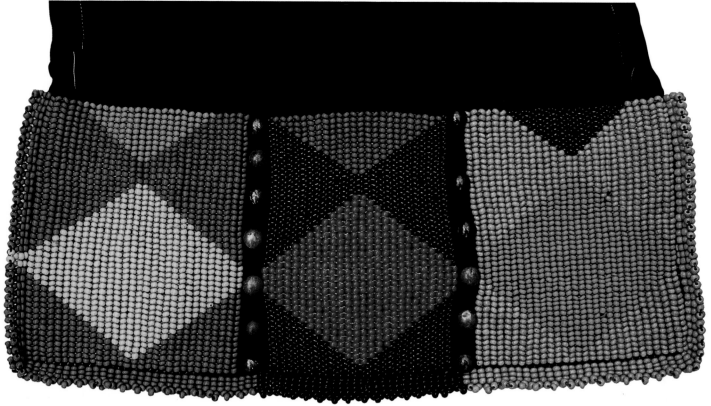

A married woman with a necklace in the *umzansi* style at Muden. Small bottles are incorporated into the necklace, either as decoration or for 'medicine' to ward off evil.

Msinga variations.
Top to bottom: Necklace from the Emabomvini clan, *c.*1980; necklet from Tugela Ferry in the Keat's Drift area; necklace from the Bathenzini clan, *c.*1950.

A young girl at the market, Keat's Drift, 1989.

A typical rural scene near Keat's Drift in the Msinga area.

That it is the younger generation who initiate these changes is borne out by the words of Mrs Hluphekile Zuma, who, in response to a query as to where styles come from, commented: 'We learned it from our mothers and our mothers learned it from their mothers. How should we know where it came from? But our daughters started making *isimodeni*.' Her daughter remarked: 'My mother calls it *isimodeni* because she is old. We call it *isilomi*.'[10] For her the style is not 'modern' but contemporary.

The feel of life in Msinga is captured by the photographs on this page. Women leave their homes to visit a market and, in so doing, dress for the occasion.

Although similar changes in style have been reported from many other areas, older styles remain and are adapted to meet the moment. This is particularly the case with the beadwork of the Nongoma area, where the emphasis placed on tradition by the king and royal family seems to ensure preservation. In any case, the multicoloured patterns of Nongoma designs (pp. 50-1) allow a good deal of leeway for experimentation, and make for spectacular decoration.

Among the identifying features of Nongoma beadwork is the diamond-shaped pattern. The shape is said to represent a shield, which symbolizes protection.

Above left: A beaded apron worn over an *isidwaba*, or leather skirt, by married women in the Nongoma area, *c.* 1950.

Below left: A second beaded apron of the kind worn by women over an *isidwaba*, *c.* 1950. Men also wear such aprons on special occasions, but on the hip.

Above right: Shoulder bands or cross belts in the distinctive Nongoma style and colours, often worn by men, *c.* 1950. A matching girdle worn by married women over a leather skirt. Both these items were bought from a diviner, *c.* 1950.

Right: Anklet in the Nongoma style and colours, worn by both men and women, *c.* 1950.

Overleaf: Girdles (*itshitshi*) worn by girls, Mahlabatini area, *c.* 1960. These belts can also be worn by unmarried men. The designs are relatively modern; they show unmarried girls, as indicated by the absence of a headdress on the stylized figure.

Beaded fertility doll from Msinga area in the *isithembu* colours, c.1970. When undergoing *memulo*, or fertility ceremonies, young girls wear their hair in long strands like those of the two dolls portrayed on this page.

Right: **A genuine beaded fertility doll in the *umzansi* colour scheme, made in Msinga for a girl during her coming-of-age ceremony, c.1970.**

A unique feature of the Msinga area is small beaded dolls referred to both in the literature and by the public as 'fertility dolls'. Although made in other parts of the country, traditional dolls are not often found in Natal and Zululand outside Msinga.

Until about thirty years ago, when they seem to have fallen somewhat from favour, Msinga dolls were made by girls for their own entertainment, or to give to lovers who sometimes hung them over their shoulders on long beaded strings. When some local women began to sell beadwork from door to door in White towns and villages these dolls experienced something of a renaissance. Because Whites associated them with fertility and the supposed mysteries of puberty ceremonies, they sold well. The fact that their form – a beaded cylinder with hair and no facial features – was alien to Western notions of a doll only added to the popular mystery surrounding them, and made them sell the faster. Although few of their purchasers recognize the identifying features, many of these dolls incorporated in their linear beading the typical colour schemes of the Msinga area.

In the early 1970s, Mrs Zuma, whose words were quoted on p. 49, began to make a line of 'traditional' dolls specifically for the tourist market. Middlemen and traders had begun to scour Msinga for beadwork and a number of local women were supplying them both with old beadwork that was eventually sold as collector's items, and with smaller necklaces and belts that could be worn as costume jewelry. *Doli*,

as they were called, joined these pieces and have become a firm favourite with the White buying public. They are sold in curio shops and even in department stores, where they are displayed with other famous 'traditional' African dolls, such as those made by Ndebele women.

Some Msinga dolls have retained their original form, but others have acquired faces, arms and even legs. Many of Mrs Zuma's dolls have now broken completely with the conventions of the past: they come in all sizes and often replicate the clothing of local people in the Msinga area. Their meaning has also changed. They no longer signal a message to a lover but speak, instead, to the desire of the tourist for an ethnic memento. For the maker, they speak of making money. These are themes that will recur in the chapters to come.

Commercial 'fertility dolls' for sale at the side of the road in Msinga, 1989.

Below: Beaded cloth doll with the 'top knot' of a married woman, made for the White market and sold door-to-door as 'fertility dolls', Msinga, *c.*1970. Genuine fertility dolls do not have facial features such as eyes and mouth.

Overleaf: It is often difficult to distinguish a genuine *ucu*, or neck ornament, from the popular Zulu 'love letter' which is made to catch the eye of tourists. These examples are all from the Nongoma and Mahlabatini areas, *c.*1960s.

The bead colours that dominated old Msinga beadwork had, and in some contexts may still have, meanings attached to them. In this manner they form a symbolic system that allows particular pieces of beadwork to speak to their audience. Older beadmakers tend to agree that in general terms white beads stand for purity and perhaps innocence, black for depth and profundity, while light blue beads indicate ripeness and fertility.

Such associations are not entirely limited to the colour of beads, for there is a well-developed system of colour symbolism in Zulu cosmology with which these 'meanings' are in substantial agreement. The situation is complicated, however, by a number of factors. In the context of beadwork, colour does not operate alone, but is affected by other issues such as the size of the beads concerned, and their placing in relation to adjacent beads. Even the material from which the beads are made – glass or plastic – may influence the message

or impact of the particular item. There are some beaded objects, furthermore, that do not carry messages at all. The style and colour of beadwork that is a fixed part of a particular costume may indicate the provenance of the wearer, but little else; and it is quite incorrect to read into the colours that are used such meanings as may exist in the case of other items.

It is into small decorative pieces of beadwork that may be given as gifts, often between lovers and to close associates, that 'messages' are usually woven. Even then, the practice is by no means universal or uniform. In some areas beadmakers deny making and sending messages in beadwork, while comparisons between the meanings given to the same colours and type of beads is far from uniform between different areas. Where messages are involved, the code tends to be locally specific and it is often only the most general message that can be 'read'. For a fuller 'reading', one has to have a

Beaded necklet with the 'letters' spelling out 'what do you doubt about me?', Bergville, *c.*1983. The maker explained that it was designed to hasten a reluctant lover to propose marriage. However, letters do not always make words or convey messages.

Right: Detail of modern beadwork belts incorporating letters and numbers.

detailed knowledge of the regional and probably the social and familial context of the beadmaker, together with the audience or person with whom she is aiming to communicate. It may be only with the help of her own interpretation that the full meaning of her work will emerge. In this sense many of the 'messages' are personal and private communications which the beadmaker might not want to be available to a wider audience. Messages of love would fall into this category, although the expression of anger at rejection or infidelity might be addressed to a wider audience.

The beadwork worn by young men and women is, as we have seen, intimately connected with courting and love. As they mature, boys attract the attentions of girls and receive beaded gifts and, in particular, strands of beads from which small squares of intricate and multicolored beadwork often hang.

These are referred to as *ucu*, a Zulu term that has been widely translated as 'love letter'. Women wear similar decorations. They are popular because they are small and a number can be worn at once, making for a colourful display. Some are more elaborate than others, with colour to enliven them, but also designs and letters. In cases where they incorporate the latter the impression is deepened that they are indeed, 'bead messages'. Often, however, the letters do not form words, or the words 'sense': they are merely part of a decorative design. In these examples, letters and words are similar to colours in that they may mean very little in themselves; one needs to know the context of their use to 'read' them. In many instances the makers cannot read or write, and have asked someone else to write a word or letters down for them to copy – and to fit as they like into their overall design.

There are, it must be stressed, only elements of truth in the belief held by many White South Africans that all beads 'tell a story'. The roots of this notion go back to the colonial past when the traditions of many Black people were misunderstood and often romanticized as evidence of the innate difference between White and Black and – so it was believed – of the essential primitiveness of the latter. In the case of beaded 'love letters', the message which the myth propagated was that those who sent them were 'savage' or 'primitive', 'Mankind's children' perhaps, who, because they could not read, had to rely on colour to transmit meaning. Blown out of all proportion, this 'message' has, however, had its positive side: it has provided the basis for much of the appeal of African beadwork and, with this, its popularity on the curio and tourist market.

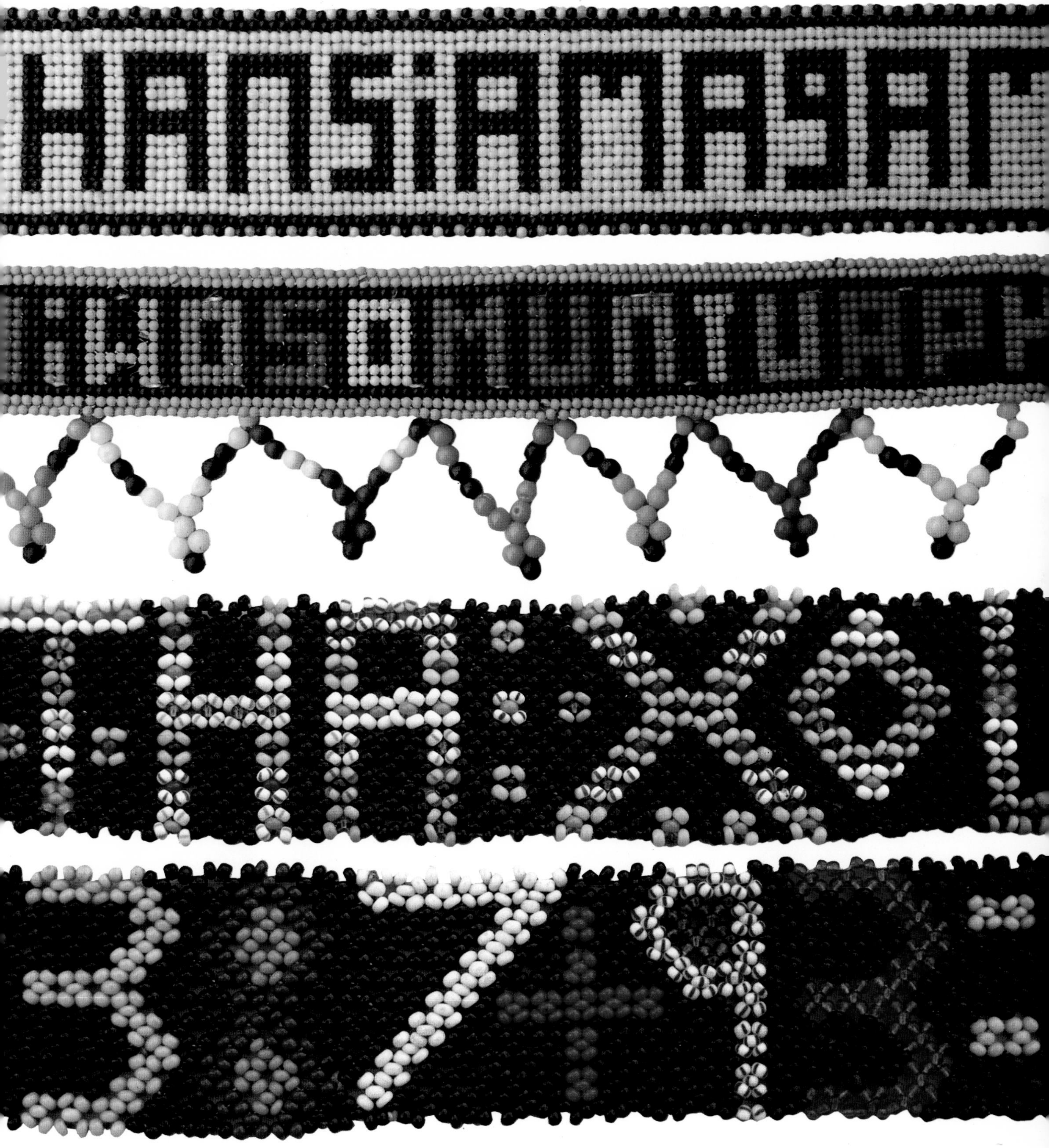

4
SPEAKING OF RELIGION

Geraldine Morcom

An early photograph, taken in 1959, shows that Shembe dress and beadwork have changed little over the years.

Yet another example of the integral role played by beadwork in contemporary dress is to be found in the religious regalia worn by women of the Nazareth Baptist Church. Often referred to as the Shembe Church after its founder and prophet Isaiah Shembe, this independent African church is thousands strong, with members coming from all over Natal and also from as far afield as Maputa and Zimbabwe. The Church is famous for its religious pilgrimages and festivals, which draw the faithful to worship at a number of holy places in Natal, and for the unique display of dress and dancing that characterize these events. Jean Morris attended the July festival of the Church in 1959, 1973 and 1989 and her photographs highlight not only the beauty and complexity of the beaded ornaments worn by worshippers on each occasion, but also a striking continuity in style.

Ibandla Lamanazaretha, or the Nazareth Baptist Church, was founded in about 1910 by the prophet Isaiah Shembe. Although he established his headquarters, known as Ekuphakameni (from the Zulu word for an elevated or high place), at Inanda near Durban, Shembe travelled widely throughout Natal, and what was then Zululand, spreading his religious message. This consisted of a unique fusion of Zulu and orthodox Christian theology, which continued to draw adherents long after his death in 1935. The leadership of the

The marital status of a woman is indicated by the elaborately beaded headband and tall headpiece unique to the Shembe. July Festival, Ekuphakameni, mid-1970s.

Black cloaks adorned with mauve pompons form part of the dance uniform of older married women belonging to the Nazareth Baptist Church. Cloaks are drawn around the shoulders out of reverence for God. July Festival, Ekuphakameni, 1972.

Young girls, not yet of marriageable age, wear short red skirts and no headdress when dancing. July Festival, Ekuphakameni, mid-1970s.

Below: **Shields and furled umbrellas are carried by married women at Shembe dances. These are used in the symbolic fight against evil. No shoes are worn at Ebuhleni, for it is a holy place. July Festival, Ebuhleni, 1989.**

church passed to the prophet's son, Johannes Galilee Shembe, whose own death was, however, followed by a succession dispute between his brother, Amos Shembe, and his son Londa. This led to a split in the church and to the establishment by Amos Shembe of a new religious centre at Ebuhleni, some 12-13 miles from Ekuphakameni. It is here that the great July festival is now held. This is a time of religious pilgrimage when the faithful build temporary homes at Ebuhleni and live and worship for the month with their leader. The days of public dancing, which are an integral part of the festival, draw hundreds of spectators and, increasingly, tourists to Ebuhleni.

The dances are indeed spectacular. Ordered groups of men and women, sometimes hundreds strong, take turns to dance and to sing the hymns of the church. Often referred to in a military

Short black skirts and headbands distinguish girls of marriageable age from those not yet ready for marriage. July Festival, Ekuphakameni, mid-1970s.

Below: Men and boys dance together, separately from women and girls. Animal skins and feathers predominate in dancing regalia worn by men and the beaded anklets and armbands are made by Shembe women. July Festival, Ekuphakameni, mid-1970s.

idiom as 'regiments', each group is dressed in a distinctive uniform indicating not only gender, but age and marital status. Women are clearly distinguished from men, while girls with their bare breasts and minuscule skirts – the traditional garb of unmarried women – stand out from the married women. The latter are clad in flowing cloaks and the heavy leather skirts and tall headdress typical of the dress of conservative Zulu matrons. Some of the younger men wear kilts, while skins and feathers dominate the dancing dress of older men.

The ambience of the dance and the inspiration for the Church regalia are drawn as much from the history and greatness of the Zulu Kingdom as from the Kingdom of Christ. In the July festival of the Shembe Church no conflict exists between the Christian message of salvation and the use of

Variations in the headdress worn by married women attending church services. July Festival, Ekuphakameni, mid-1970s.

Below: Spectacular elongated headdress seen at the Shembe festival. Respect is shown to God through the use of these headdresses within the Church.

Right, top to bottom: The shape of the headpiece indicates the origin of the wearer. Tall headdresses are worn by those who live north of the Tugela River.

Headcovering of wool lightly bound with cotton thread.

A married woman declares her Msinga origin in the red, green and black beads and in the brass studs which form part of her headband.

Headdresses worn by married women in dance attire at the July Festival, Ebuhleni, 1989.

Far left: Round headpieces are worn by those living south of the Tugela river.

Left: A wide lacy necklet of beads is worn with the dance uniform of married women. A pompon of ostrich feathers adorns the headdress.

Below: A cascade of beaded strings from head to shoulder is part of the dance attire for the married women.

Beaded wristbands and broad bands of beadwork used to decorate headdresses. Designs in colour are set against a typical white background. The Church of the Nazarites, founded by Isaiah Shembe in 1911, has developed the secular meaning of beads to include spiritual meaning, incorporating the cross as a design motif.

Typical Shembe cross-like patterns are clearly evident in one of these pieces. July Festival, Ebuhleni, 1989.

The top design is called *ufish* because of its fish-like shape, while the lower design is said to resemble a shield.

Headband and anklets in matching colours and design.

Zulu tradition. Instead they are celebrated together with the utmost ceremony and reverence. It is predominantly in the costumes of women and girls that beadwork proliferates and is used not only as decoration, but to identify the faithful and incorporate them as worshippers into the body and organizational structures of the Church.

A distinctive feature of Shembe beadwork is a predominance of white beads forming the ground for ornate and exquisitely coloured geometric patterns. The symbolism of the white ground is drawn from Christian notions of purity, as well as from positive associations that white has in traditional Zulu cosmology. The designs are personally selected by the wearer and, while no specific language of colour exists, the choice of colour and pattern are often a pointer to the geographical area from which the wearer comes. Latterly, new designs – making use of an increasing number of colours and patterns – are created almost annually and exist alongside the older designs, which are usually characterized by their

Beadwork for sale to those taking part in the July Festival, Ebuhleni, 1989.

A married woman making beadwork to sell. Ebuhleni, July 1989.

primary colours and a network of cross-like symbols. A range of translucent and highly lustred beads are used, in particular, to create patterns that are reminiscent of modern fabric designs but may have, in themselves, little overt religious symbolism. They exist, it seems, purely to please the eye and to give expression to the skill of the maker in the service and worship of her Saviour. Sometimes images drawn from everyday life – for instance, a razor blade or a fish – are used. Alternatively, letters may decorate an item of beadwork or an image such as a Zulu shield. This clearly identifies the traditional ethos of the Church. The beads that are preferred for religious regalia are of the imported glass variety and are generally small. They are woven into belts, headbands, anklets and wrist decorations and are also used to decorate the cloths worn by women to cover their dancing skirts.

As elsewhere in the region, it is the women and girls who are responsible for making beadwork. While it is sometimes for their own use that they weave, the more skilled among their

number produce items for sale and take orders from people who have never learned the art of beadmaking. It is here that originality as well as skill may well be the deciding factor in attracting buyers. Young girls often experiment and practise making their own beadwork in groups, and it is one of their pastimes while living at Ebuhleni for the month of July.

The wearing and, to some extent, the weaving of beads are a religious obligation for women of the Church. Beadwork thus acts as a marker not only of religious, but also of sectarian piety. Although superficially similar to much traditional beadwork, the patterns and colour combinations of Shembe beadwork are immediately recognized both by members of the Church from all over the country, and by most non-church attenders. It is, in fact, by the style of their beadwork that Church members distinguish themselves, on the one hand, from traditionalists who also wear beadwork and, on the other hand, from Christians who belong to other churches but who eschew the use of beadwork in their church uniforms.

The ornately beaded frontal apron and matching band of beadwork worn with it are standard features of the dance uniform of young adolescent girls. Designs and colours are the personal choice of the wearer. July Festival, Ebuhleni, 1989.

A basic tenet of the Nazareth Baptist Church is that God is worshipped through dancing and collective prayer. At Ebuhleni each activity occurs in a specially demarcated area and members wear uniforms that are peculiar to each activity. These were originally prescribed by Isaiah Shembe following a number of prophetic visions. For this reason, while elaborations in the details of uniforms occur and new bead colours and designs appear each year, the basic style of the uniforms, as well as the distinctions they mark between married women and adolescent girls, have remained essentially unchanged since his time. The emphasis that the prophet placed on traditional Zulu values and forms of organization in building his church, and the manner in which he integrated traditional dance and dress into the worship of the Christian God, set his Church aside from all similar religious movements in the region. Above all, he ensured that both dress and dance are integral to Nazarite prayer and worship.

The fact that prayer and dancing are distinguished means that most Church members have at least two distinct uniforms, and as they grow older and marry, their dancing uniform will change. Young girls of marriageable age may have as many as five uniforms and, while decorative beaded arm and ankle bands may be worn with those based on Western dress, only one incorporates beadwork in the traditional

Primary colours and the extended cross-like motif form the basis of the design in this frontal apron. July Festival, Ebuhleni, 1989.

Translucent and highly lustred beads in a range of colours and patterns have been used to decorate this frontal apron. July Festival, Ebuhleni, 1989.

Right: An outfit of dance clothing worn by a girl of marriageable age. Beadwork forms the bulk of this uniform. A broad band of beadwork, mainly in white with small blocks of colour, covers the buttock area while narrower bands are worn around the waist and chest. The frontal apron is a reminder of traditional adornment; the beaded headband and short black skirt speak of the girl's social age. The shield and the umbrella are used symbolically in dance to fend off evil. Ebuhleni, July 1989.

Right: Senior man in a leopard-skin cape. Men carry cowhide shields and sticks decorated with animal hair. The shields used by men are usually larger than those carried by women. July Festival, Ebuhleni 1989.

Framed photograph of the prophet Isaiah Shembe, referred to as *ifoto* and worn for spiritual protection, *c.* 1984.

A married woman with a prayer mat under her arm is dressed in the prayer uniform *Umnazaretha*. Prayer mats are used during Church services and are often decorated with small block-shape patterns in coloured wool. Ebuhleni, July 1989.

Right: A Nazarite family dressed in white cloth smocks. Prayer uniforms are worn by men, women and children of all ages. Ebuhleni, July 1989.

Women seated on the ground for late afternoon prayer. July Festival, Ekuphakameni, mid-1970s.

manner. This is shown on pp. 68-9 and is worn for the public dancing at the July festival.

The basic prayer uniform worn by all Church members consists of a white cloth smock, the style of which differs slightly for men and women and for people of different ages. Even infants and pre-adolescent children must adopt this smock for prayer. It is referred to by the name of the Church – the umNazaretha – and it is the first and most basic symbol of both their Christian and Nazarite faith. Men wear the smock over their trousers and, with the possible exception of a beaded necklace carrying a picture of the prophet and referred to as *ifoto*, their uniform is plain. In addition to their smocks, women wear a white cloth around their shoulders as a sign of respect to God and to the head of the

Church, who himself leads communal prayers. Young girls wear a similar cloth around their heads. In the case of married women, the prayer uniform is complemented by the adoption of the headpiece of a traditional Zulu wife, which is decorated with a beaded band in the design and colours of her choice. Additional squares of beadwork may be attached to the headdress and most women wear beaded anklets above their bare feet. When going to prayer they carry a woven mat, which is yet another symbol of traditional rural life. As a reminder of church routine, married women wear a black clothband around their waists. This is referred to as U14, and it is a reminder of the meetings held on the 14th of each month in their home districts. Like men they may wear *ifoto* with their prayer uniform.

It is in women's dancing attire that beadwork comes into its own. Not only do they sport their decorated headdresses and anklets, but also the edge of the cloth that covers their skin skirt has two rows of intricate beadwork. They usually wear a wide beaded belt, a striking lace-like cascade of beadwork, falling from the headdress to the shoulders, and a wide necklace. As the photographs of individual women on pp. 64-5 show, although the essential elements of the dress are standard, there is ample room for individuality in the displays of beadwork. For dancing, a black cloak, decorated with mauve pompons, is worn, while yet another pompon adorns the front of the headdress. To complete the dancing outfit, women carry a furled umbrella and shield – symbolic weapons in the fight against evil.

**Zulu men in slow rhythmic dance.
Ekuphakameni, mid -1970s.**

Unmarried girls are divided into three categories: those before adolescence who may not yet join the dancing as a distinctive regiment; the very young adolescents; and those who are older and of marriageable age. The second group wear short red skirts when dancing, together with elaborately beaded breast bands and a distinctive frontal apron which is usually a kaleidoscope of pattern and colour. The older girls are marked by their black cloth skirts, which foreshadow the cowhide marriage skirt, and by wide headbands in bright geometric designs. Like the married women, they carry a black umbrella in their right hand and a shield in their left, which are used in the context of the dance as 'religious weapons' with which to fend off evil. No shoes are worn when dancing, for Ebuhleni is a Holy Place.

While Ebuhleni and, long before it, Ekuphakameni have come to be sacred places where the faithful gather with their leader to renew and express their faith for the duration of the July festival, they are also the home of thousands of people who need to be housed and fed. Opportunities for informal money-making abound and church members have not been slow to capitalize on them. Indeed, Isaiah Shembe extolled the religious virtue of hard work and preached that the sabbath was a day of rest only in

Shielding her face from the sun, a newly married woman wears a deep purple cloak – in the place of a white one – with her prayer smock. This cloak is worn until she has had at least two children.

relation to a week of toil. The current leader of the Church, Amos Shembe, specifically encourages all, and women in particular, to use their hands to make items of traditional craft for their own use and to sell.

Because many members of the Church have had little education and, once again particularly in the case of women and girls, find it difficult to secure employment, the making and selling of beadwork provides another welcome source of income. It is not only beadwork, however, that may be lucrative: women from predominantly conservative rural backgrounds make headdresses and cowhide skirts, while those from mission areas and Christian homes offer their services as seamstresses. A few bring grass prayer mats from their rural homes and sell them. Men assist in the building of the temporary homes and both men and women run shack shops and wayside stalls offering food and drink, as well as religious memorabilia.

While Ebuhleni is a hive of economic activity during July, women have to survive for the rest of the year as well. Many once again put their beadmaking skills to use in producing curio beadwork for sale to tourists. They frequent the streets outside plush Durban hotels and some have stalls in beachfront markets. The story of this trade is the subject of the next chapter.

5
SPEAKING OF FASHION AND ART

A hat made in the Valley of a Thousand Hills for the tourist or fashion market, and sold through the African Art Centre in the mid -1980s.

It is not only women of the Nazareth Baptist Church who have found that there is a market for Zulu beadwork. Two other lucrative arenas have opened up for its sale: these are the country-wide tourist and curio trade and an international demand for high-fashion beaded jewelry. In addition, the art world has discovered contemporary African beadwork, leading to the purchase of specific items by galleries, museums and private collectors from around the world. Although apparently separate, the opportunities created in all these fields shade into each other and the same craftswomen often supply all of them: indeed, it is the combined and various demands from all that have stimulated indigenous creativity and have led to the renaissance in beadworking 'traditions' and skills to which this volume is a tribute.

Beadwork and other craft items, such as baskets and wood carvings, have long been peddled at the side of many roads and highways. Over the last decade an increasing number of entrepreneurs, both Black and White, have realized that a growing market exists for a wide range of goods that have an 'ethnic flavour'. As tourism has become 'big business', so 'traditional African culture' and in Natal, Zulu culture in particular, has come to be an increasing selling point in the brochures that lure both local holiday makers and overseas tourists to the region.

A cap made for dancing, Nongoma, c. 1950.

A profusion of curio beadwork for sale on the Durban beachfront during the 1970s. Predominant are simple geometric designs in primary colours and the ever popular Zulu 'love letters'.

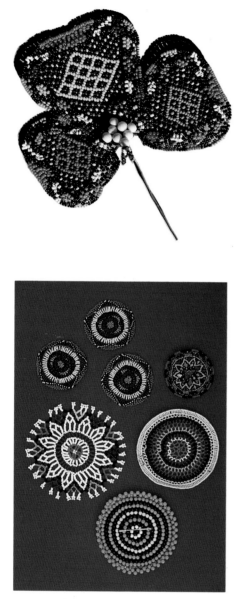

Decorative headdress pin, or *izipeletu*, Ndwedwe, Valley of a Thousand Hills, *c.* 1989.

Right: **A wide range of curio beadwork is sold at stalls in the famous Umgababa markets, south of Durban. Examples range from medicine horns to 'Shaka's stabbing spear' and the more practical beaded salad servers. These items date from the 1980s.**

Modern coasters (*above*) made on a wire frame in a manner similar to the rondels (*below*) made to pin on skirts and headdresses. Eshowe, *c.* 1980.

A number of the major tourist routes in Natal pass through rural areas that are the homes of Black peasant farmers. As traffic increased women and children began to sell local fruit and vegetables at the roadside and, in cases where the land farmed by women ran down to the road, it was a simple matter to set up stalls and combine selling with other household tasks. In some instances, groups of women collected at sites with fine views and at crossroads to sell their wares. A few happened to be wearing beaded necklaces and bracelets, and oldtimers recall how, in the 1940s and 1950s, motorists were often more interested in these than in the fruit that was offered for sale: 'they pulled our beads out of our blouses and wanted to buy them – and they also asked for the baskets we carried the fruit in … so some of us brought beadwork to sell. I once took some strings of beads one day and they were gone in a minute.'

Enterprising women collected baskets, mats and beadwork from their neighbours to sell at the roadside, and in some areas what amounted to a small industry developed to keep mushrooming wayside stalls provided with goods. The type of beadwork that reached the roadside was at first simple necklaces and bracelets which had not needed too many beads, or too much time, to make. Some women were prepared to sell items for which they no

longer had much use, but in time, like the women of the Shembe community, most developed a range of beaded jewelry specifically for the passing trade. They learned from experience what motorists would buy – and what they were prepared to pay – and adjusted their production accordingly.

It was not only beadmakers who realized that money could be made from the sale of curios. Entrepreneurs with a keen sense of business and the contacts to market the finished product have set up workshops and cottage industries to produce beadwork in bulk. A good example of this is Bekithunga, which is situated near Eshowe in central Zululand in an area where traditional beadwork flourishes. Local women are provided with beads, which they make into a standard line of curio items – belts, necklaces, beaded assegais and spears (see p. 77; 78, *top*). Some women work at home and are paid piecemeal, while others come to a central workshop where they weave under the guidance of the management. Although they are working on set pieces, there is room for individual inspiration in the details of the patterns used to decorate the curio range. The advantage of working for the project is that women are assured a regular income in an area where little work is available for them. Since they live far from town and their homes do not abut a major highway, it is unlikely

Beadwork bands in geometric designs decorate the handles of ceremonial spears made during the 1980s at Bekithunga, near Shakaland.

Below: Costumed dancers at Shakaland entertain guests with a superlative display of traditional dancing, 1990.

Beaded hip belt made with large modern plastic beads at Shakaland, 1990.

that they could easily negotiate the sale of their own beadwork. It is the management of Bekithunga that allows them to 'speak of money' from their beadworking skills.

Situated near to Bekithunga, and once closely associated with it, is yet another commercial venture which promotes an interest in – and the sale of – curio beadwork. Designed to capture a slice of the growing overseas tourist market, Shakaland takes its inspiration from Disneyland in providing visitors with a 'real Zulu' experience. The sets of a well-known film and television spectacular, 'Shaka Zulu', have been extended to provide overnight accommodation in what looks like a Zulu dwelling hut, but one which has electricity, hot and cold running water and a bathroom en suite! The highlight of the stay is a lesson in Zulu history, a visit to a Zulu homestead and, after dinner (slightly 'Zulu style'), a display of 'traditional dancing'. The experience is packaged in the trappings of stereotypical Zulu culture – or what the tourists come to believe is Zulu culture. A major part of this illusion is produced by the skilful use of traditional dress in which beadwork dazzles the eye. To complete the experience, items of beadwork similar to those worn by the 'maidens' and 'warriors' of Shakaland can be purchased in the curio store on the way out.

Demonstrating beadmaking at Shakaland, 1990.

As some of the smaller roadside markets grew and diversified, they became centres of local and even regional trade. Producers were joined by full-time traders who developed vast networks of suppliers from whom they bought and ordered stock. The most famous indigenous curio markets are situated at Umgababa, some 25 miles south of Durban. They are entirely the preserve of women and attract hundreds of holiday makers and tourists each year.

Umgababa has, at times, housed over four hundred traders. Each woman owns and runs her stall and collects her wares from producers living throughout Natal and KwaZulu. Middlemen from as far afield as Swaziland and Maputo deliver goods regularly and, in holiday time, the market is a bustling centre, not only of trade, but also of entertainment and fun. Tourists browse at will through the stalls and wander between the grass mats and clay pots which spill out of the stall entrances. Older women make craft outside their stalls, and this assures most buyers that they are getting the 'genuine article'. For those who are not so fussy, there are hundreds of cheap goods – including beadwork – that are imported from as far afield as India and Taiwan. Although most stalls at Umgababa stock some beadwork, traders tend to specialize in either 'traditional' pieces

Ricksha pullers on the Durban beach front in the early 1980s, with ornate beadwork reminiscent of the Nongoma and Mahlabatini areas. The medal with a date on it indicates that the wearer won the prize for the best costume of the year.

which they claim are 'original' (and so expensive) or in cheaper curios such as the beaded spears, medicine bottles and the ever popular 'love letters' (p. 77). Quick to sell are necklaces in colours that complement contemporary fashion. As one trader explained: 'Most visitors like to see beads in what we call 'Zulu' colours, that is plain red, blue and white in squares and triangles … but they also like the new jewelry in pink and mauve and orange … it goes with their dresses. The overseas visitors get excited about Zulu things like Shaka's stabbing spear – we sold hundreds after the film … and they love to take a medicine bottle home. I always stock lots of them. The South African visitors usually want something they can use and so I get wooden salad spoons and tell my beadmakers to decorate the handles.'

While tourists are drawn to Umgababa, beadsellers are also drawn to all the places where tourists and holidaymakers collect. The sight of women and youngsters hawking beads, baskets and mats is a feature of most Natal holiday resorts. The Durban beach front, with its continual melee of people from all over the country, if not the world, is a prime example of this. In fact curio sellers, together with the famous ricksha pullers in their heavily beaded costumes, provide a touch of the exotic and of 'primitive Africa' to the whole beach front area. For this reason they are as welcome to the city fathers as are the tourists themselves. The craft sellers have in fact been provided with stalls

and, what was once a purely informal trade carried on by a few enterprising women, has been all but incorporated into the formal tourist industry.

While there is always money to be made peddling relatively inexpensive bead curios, more substantial profits come from supplying the demand for, on the one hand, up-market costume or fashion jewelry and on the other, beadwork that qualifies as contemporary African art. In these arenas it is seldom individual Black women who are the entrepreneurs: rather it is, as at Bekithunga and Shakaland, White business people who have the capital, economic experience and established commercial networks to organize and carry through large-scale marketing strategies. Some of these are in the business solely for the profit it brings them, but others are the representatives of philanthropic and development organizations whose objective is to fight the country's widespread poverty. A major target in the case of beadwork production is the category of rural women who have few other sources of income. Important among the philanthropic organizations is the Mdukutshani Beadwork Project based at Tugela Ferry in the Msinga area, which specializes in fashion jewelry, and the African Art Centre in Durban, which has pioneered a novel form of beaded art. In other parts of the country large organizations such as Operation Hunger have done similar work and have popularized the art of Southern African beadwork as a whole.

Beadwork, along with plastic dolls dressed as Zulu married women, for sale on the Durban beach front in the late 1980s.

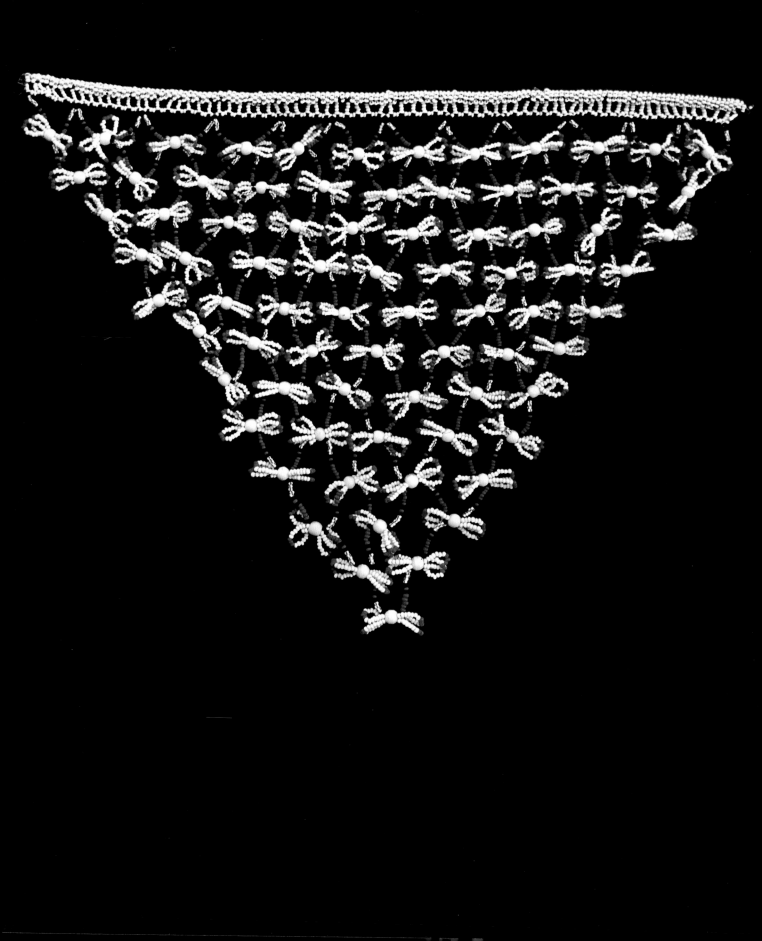

An unusual modern triangular neckpiece with beaded knots, Ndwedwe area, Valley of a Thousand Hills.

The old and the new.
Above: A modern fashion necklace made at the Mdukutshani project, *c.* 1982.

Below: The 'original' from which the modern necklace is derived – a shoulder band from Msinga, *c.* 1960.

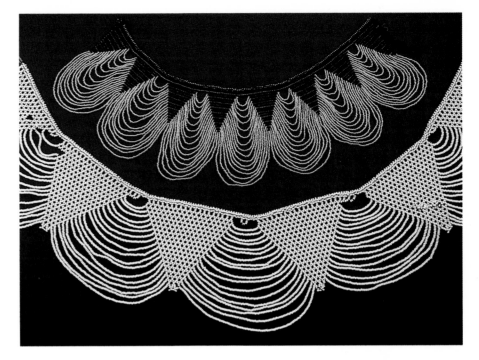

Mdukutshani was the creation of Crena Bond and was part of a wider development project run in the Msinga area by a church-based group under the leadership of her husband, Neil Alcock. It was the first beadwork project to import beads in fashion colours and to plan its range to suit the international fashion market. Taking these new and lustrous beads the women of the area produced a range of strikingly original costume jewelry which gained instant popularity with overseas buyers and the fashion houses of America and Paris (pp. 83-5). Orders flooded in and the majority of the work done by project members is still exported.

Rural women who visit the city in order to sell their curio beadwork invariably make the rounds of likely buyers: some remain in the beachfront area selling directly to the public, others sell to curio shops and some have discovered in the African Art Centre both a buyer and promoter. Started in the 1960s, the Art Centre was a project of the South African Institute for Race Relations, which is a voluntary organization devoted to promoting inter-racial contact and understanding. The Art Centre set out to encourage and assist Black artists and craftspeople to develop their talents and, by providing a gallery to show their work, assisted in drawing it to the notice of the buying public. Beadwork of the highest quality soon became a feature of the gallery's stock and a regular clientele of both buyers and beadmakers developed around the person of Jo Thorpe, the first co-ordinator of the Art Centre. Under her guidance the Centre established a policy of buying only the best contemporary beadwork, and it is here that collectors and museum curators come to select pieces that are either 'genuine' or avant garde. Into the latter category fall the now famous bead and cloth sculptures.

High fashion necklaces from the Mdukutshani
project sold during the 1980s and early 1990s.
Note the translucent glass beads in muted
fashion colours.

Above left: Baby in a coffin by Sizakhele Mchunu. The grief of the artist at the loss of her own baby is reflected in this sculpture.

Above: An African interpretation of the crucifixion by Sizakhele Mchunu.

Left: Sizakhele Mchunu displays her bead sculptures at the African Art Centre in 1989.

Buck by Hlaleleni Mlaba.

A large doll dressed in clothing very similar to that worn by the maker, MaHlambisa, on important occasions. African Art Centre, 1988.

About twenty years ago Thembi Mchunu, one of the Art Centre's regular suppliers made a small beaded cloth doll. Encouraged by Jo Thorpe, she and other women subsequently developed a genre of beaded cloth figures which have now become not only popular with a wide range of individual buyers, but are also sought after by museums and art galleries both in South Africa and abroad. Among the most famous exponent of the new art was Sizakhele Mchunu, who – with her co-wife Celani Nojieza – has made hundreds of beaded figures and tableaux depicting the life and experiences of rural Black women. Sizakhele's sculptures, first of a baby in a coffin, and later – in a series – of women grieving for children who have

died, have touched the hearts of observers around the world. In sharp contrast are the joyous sculptures of children and of mothers playing with their babies for which she and many other beadmakers are justly famous, as well as the popular bird and animal sculptures at which they also excel. A feature of all bead sculptures is a minute attention to detail, and the beadwork in which the figures are dressed is an exact replica of that worn by the makers and their neighbours.

Summarizing our review of contemporary Zulu beadwork so far, we may distinguish at least three parallel traditions. The first represents the ongoing response to changing internal demands for aesthetic expression and, in the case of dress, social differentiation.

The beadwork of the Nazareth Church is an example of the latter, but the contemporary beadwork made by women from such conservative areas as Msinga is often equally elaborate and beautiful. The second tradition consists of relatively standard 'curio' items produced for the tourist and fashion markets, and the third includes creative and original extensions to the art of beadwork such as bead sculptures and also the Msinga fertility dolls described in Chapter 3. In many cases the same beadmakers are involved in the production of all or most of these beadwork forms, merely suiting their style to the purpose in hand. Of such skill and creativity is an art form made and given life.

6
SPEAKING OF TRADITION AND NATIONALISM

We draw this photographic essay to a close on a high note and one which indicates that contemporary beadwork 'speaks' not only of personal adornment and money-making, but also, on the appropriate occasion, of nationalism and ethnic identity.

A spectacular event in the Zulu ceremonial calendar is the Umhlanga or Reed Dance, which is celebrated annually at the royal capital near Nongoma. The ceremony is held under the patronage of King Goodwill Zwelithini who, it is said, revived a traditional event which lapsed after the dismantling of the Zulu kingdom in the reign of King Mpande. The Umhlanga can best be described as a national dance in which young women come to the capital from all over the kingdom to perform before the monarch and his assembled guests. The King uses the occasion to speak directly to the youth of the nation and, of late, it has been used also as a political platform from which both he and other prominent members of the Government make pronouncements of wider political import. In 1992, when the photographs reproduced here were taken, the guests of honour included the heads of state of neighbouring territories and the consular representatives from a number of overseas countries. Far from being an event of purely ceremonial importance restricted to one section of the community, the Umhlanga has thus come to be an occasion of national and

An unmarried girl displaying modern beadwork in the green and black colours and diamond-shaped 'shield' motif of the Nongoma area, 1992.

Men in ceremonial dress at the Umhlanga ceremony, 1992. Panels of beadwork in the unmistakable Nongoma style are worn by the central figure.

A man from Msinga with a contemporary beaded collar in the *isithembu* style, 1992.

diplomatic significance. It is also an occasion of grandeur and beauty.

The dance is held in Spring. Girls come to the capital to cut the long reeds used in the building of houses and for the fences of various royal residences. The emphasis is on virginity and good behaviour and the girls are throughout referred to as maidens or virgins. The older women, who are in control, are said to instruct the girls in maidenly behaviour and the King invariably reinforces this message in his address to them and to the nation. Songs, some old and others composed for the occasion, are sung as the girls carry the reeds to the capital and, followed by regiments of men, as they process to the dancing arena. After the speeches they demonstrate their dancing skill before the assembled guests. In 1992 they were put on their mettle by the rivalry which developed between them and groups of visiting girls from Swaziland and Ciskei, who performed their own dancing routines.

The girls at the Umhlanga – often as many as 4,000 – are dressed in the finest of dancing costume and this is matched and complemented by the regalia of older women and of men. Beadwork abounds and is, indeed, the

Colourful rope belts worn by an unmarried girl from the Mahlabatini area, 1992.

A rope belt of a young unmarried girl. The predominance of white beads is a feature both of the Eshowe area and of Shembe beadwork, 1992.

A disciplined burst of colour in the typical motif of the Nongoma area, 1992.

Twin girls from the Nongoma area wearing costumes made in the 'new style' of green, black and yellow modern plastic beads, 1992.

Some of the four thousand unmarried girls who came up the hillside to present the Umhlanga reeds to the King in 1992.

Earlier that morning the girls had gone down to the river to collect the Umhlanga reeds.

major feature of most dancing costumes. But it is not only dancers who wear beadwork: many of the guests who sit on the royal stand, and most of the invited speakers from the royal house and the KwaZulu government, wear – if not full traditional dress – such beadwork ornaments as they possess. The predominance of beaded decorations, besides the ceremonial itself, is the most striking feature of the event. Even the costumes of men, in which at first sight cowhide and feathers seem to figure largely, are decorated with beadwork. In the costumes of both dancers and spectators glass and plastic beads complement each other and beautiful traditional pieces are worn side by side with curio beadwork. This eclectic use of beaded decorations, drawn from many contexts, 'speaks' of a love of display and an untrammelled sense of both beauty and occasion. The girls are for the most part bare breasted, and they wear the short skirts that we have seen are typical of the unmarried. Within their ranks, pre-adolescent and adolescent girls are distinguished from older girls approaching marriage, who are dressed in longer skirts. The matrons in charge of

proceedings wear their skin skirts and headdresses and, as with the young girls, they are easily identified by the style of their beadwork. In the 1992 ceremony, the young girls of the Nazareth Baptist Church stood out clearly among the hundreds of dancers, as did the older women of the church, who sat in the audience wearing Shembe beadwork, with its typical geometric patterns on a pure white ground. The beadwork of the Nongoma area was also much in evidence both on the dancing arena and among the important guests on the stands.

The ambience of the Umhlanga is unmistakably that of 'tradition', and this is expressed both in the massed dancing and in the costumes, especially the beadwork of the participants. Many of the dancers are drawn from the ranks of traditionalists, but others have adopted traditional dress for the occasion as a symbol of their common identity as Zulu speakers. On other occasions the wearing of what is seen as 'traditional African' dress may signal a wider Black South African identity, but at Nongoma, the 'traditional' capital of the old Zulu Empire, it is 'Zuluness'

which is celebrated – and fostered. Thus are the traditions of the past revived, reworked and even created to serve political ends: in this case, a vibrant nationalism which speaks predominantly of, and to, the contemporary political scene.

Epitomizing the above are ambiguities, such as the fact that 'tradition' is spoken of both in the adoption of old beadwork styles and in the noticeable use of modern green and yellow plastic beads, doubtless to represent, in this context, the colours of the ruling Inkatha Freedom Party. We know this because we are at Nongoma in the heart of modern KwaZulu. In another context, the same colours might well be adopted and combined with others by their rivals, the ruling African National Congress.

If anything, this odyssey should have taught us that where beadwork is concerned, meaning – as much as beauty – lies in the eye of the beholder, and bead symbols speak with different voices to different people. Therein lies their appeal in the contemporary world, with its divided, yet often overlapping, identities and loyalties.

This photographic essay is offered as a tribute to the beadmakers of KwaZulu, who have built on the beauty and skills of the past, but also capitalized on the opportunities of the present. Their art is not static and, to the extent that they seek inspiration from tradition, they use it to speak in a language which appears to be both quintessentially African and yet, at the same time, universal in its appeal.

Above: **His Majesty King Goodwill Zwelithini kaBhekuzulu, monarch of the Zulu nation, addressing the people attending the Umhlanga ceremony, 1992.**

Respected guests wearing typical Shembe headdresses, seated at the side of the Royal stand, observing the ceremony, 1992.

A praise-singer, or *imbongi*, at the 1992 Umhlanga ceremony.

Young women listen to the King's address after presenting their Umhlanga reeds, 1992. They are dressed in beadwork from Nongoma with its distinctive green and black colour combination and diamond- or 'shield'-shaped geometric motif. Shoulder bands can be worn by men and unmarried women.

A magnificent complex triple wrap
featuring the colours and geometric
patterns of the Nongoma area, 1992.

NOTES ON THE TEXT

1	Stuart and Malcolm, 1986: 49
2	Stuart and Malcolm, 1986: 40
3	Stuart and Malcolm, 1986: 77
4	Stuart and Malcolm, 1986: 73
5	Cory, 1926: 61
6	Cory, 1926: 43
7	Cory, 1926: 54
8	Angas, 1849: 63
9	Jolles, 1993
10	Jolles, 1983: 52-3

BIBLIOGRAPHY

CHAPTER 1

Angas, G.F. (1849) *The Kafirs Illustrated* A facsimile reprint of the original 1849 edition of hand-coloured lithographs. Cape Town: A.A Balkemia

Carey, M. (1986) *Beads and beadwork of East and South Africa* UK: Shire Publications

Cory, Sir Geo. E., ed. (1926) *The diary of the Rev. Francis Owen, M.A.* Cape Town: The Van Riebeeck Society

Filter, H. and Bourquin, S. (1986) *Paulina Dlamini, servant of two kings* Pietermaritzburg: Natal University Press

Gardiner, A.F. (1836) *Narrative of a Journey to the Zoolu country* London: William Crofts

Klopper, S. (1986) 'George French Angas's (re)presentation of the Zulu in *The Kafirs Illustrated' South African Cultural History* 3: 63-73

Maylam, P. (1989) *A history of the African People of South Africa: From the early Iron Age to the 1970s* Cape Town: David Phillip

Saitowitz, S.J. (n.d.) *19th Century glass trade-beads from two Zulu royal residences* Unpublished MA Thesis, University of Cape Town

Stuart, J. and Malcolm, D. (1986) *The diary of Henry Francis Fynn* Pietermaritzburg: Natal University Press

Webb, C. and Wright, J. (1977) *The Stuart Archives* Vol. 1, Pietermaritzburg: Natal University Press

CHAPTER 2

Berglund, A. (1976) *Zulu Thought Patterns and Symbolism* London: Hurst

Klopper, S. (1989) 'Ten years of collecting (1979-1989)' *Catalogue: Standard Bank Foundation Collection of African art* Johannesburg: University of the Witwatersrand

Krige, E.J. (1950) *The Social System of the Zulus* Pietermaritzburg: Shuter & Shooter

Vilikazi, A. (1957) 'A reserve from within' *African Studies* 16, 93-101

CHAPTER 3

Grossert, J. (1968) *Art Education and Zulu Crafts* 2 Vols. Pietermaritzburg: Shuter & Shooter

Jolles, F. (1991) 'Interfaces between Oral and Literate societies: Contracts, runes and beadwork' *Oral Tradition and Innovation: New wine in old bottles?* Sienaert, E.R., Bell, A.N. and Lewis, M. (eds) Durban: Natal University Oral Documentation Research Centre

Kiernan, J.P. (1991) 'Wear'n'tear and repair: The colour coding of mystical mending in Zulu Zionist churches' *Africa* 61(1), 26-39

Levinsohn, R. (1979) 'Symbolic significance of traditional Zulu beadwork' *Black Art* 3,4, 29-35

Mthethwa, B.N. (1988) 'Decoding Zulu beadwork' *Oral Tradition and Innovation: New wine in old bottles?* Sienaert, E.R. et al. op. cit.

Ngubane, H. (1977) *Body and Mind in Zulu medicine: an ethnography of health and disease in Nyuswa-Zulu thought and practise* London: Academic Press

Preston-Whyte, E.M. and Thorpe, J. (1990) 'Ways of seeing, ways of buying; Images of tourist art and culture expression in contemporary beadwork' *African Art in Southern Africa* Hammond-Tooke, W.D. and Nettleton, A. (eds) Johannesburg: A.B. Donker

Schoeman, H.S. (1968a) 'A preliminary report on traditional beadwork in the Mkhwanzi area of the Maputuland district Zululand' *African Studies* 27,2 Part One, 57-81

Schoeman, H.S. (1968b) 'A preliminary report on traditional beadwork in the Mkhwanzi area of the Maputuland district Zululand' *African Studies* 27,3 Part Two, 107-133

Twala, R.G. (1958) 'Beads as regulating the social life of the Zulu and Swazi' *African Studies* 10, 3, 113-123

Winters, Y.E. (1988) 'Contemporary traditionalist Bhaca and Khuze beadwork from the Southern Natal/KwaZulu area' *South African Museum Bulletin* 18(2), 47-52

CHAPTER 4

Becken, H.J. (1965) 'On the Holy Mountain: A visit to the New Year's Festival of the Nazareth Church on Mount Nhlangakazi' *Journal of Religion in Africa* 1, 138-149

Becken, H.J. (1978) 'Ekuphameni Revisited' *Journal of Religion in Africa* 9(3), 161-172

Oosthuizen, C.G. (1967) *The Theology of a South African Messiah* Leiden: Brill

Oosthuizen, C.G. (1983) 'The Shembe Movement and the Zulu World View' *The Journal of the University of Durban Westville* 4(2), 7-24

Sundkler, B.G.M. (1961)(1948) *Bantu Prophets in South Africa* London: Oxford University Press

Sundkler, B.G.M. (1965) 'Chief and Prophet in Zululand and Swaziland' *African Systems of Thought* London: Oxford University Press

Sundkler, B.G.M. (1976) *Zulu Zion and Some Swazi Zionists* London: Oxford University Press

Vilakazi, A.; Mthethwa, B. and Mpanza, M. (1986) *Shembe: The Revitalization of African Society* Braamfontein: Skotaville Publishers

CHAPTER 5

Jolles, F. (1993) 'Traditional Zulu beadwork of the Msinga area' *African Arts* January, 42-102

Preston-Whyte, E.M. (1988) 'For sale or for use: A typology of Zulu beadwork' *South African Museums Bulletin* 18(2), 59-74

Preston-Whyte, E.M. and Thorpe, J. (1990) op. cit.

Preston-Whyte, E.M. (1991) 'Petty trading at Umgababa: Mere survival or the road to accumulation?' *South Africa's informal economy* Preston-Whyte, E.M. and Rogerson, C. (eds) Cape Town: Oxford University Press

CHAPTER 6

De Haas, M. and Zulu, P. (1991) *Ethnicity and Nationalism in Post-Apartheid South Africa : The case of Natal and the 'Zulus'* Paper presented at the American Anthropological Association's 90th Annual meeting in Chicago

Kuper, H. (1947) *An African Aristocracy* London: Oxford University Press

BEADWORK SUPPLIERS

Anyone wishing to order beads directly from South Africa should contact one of the following projects, most of which are aimed at creating income-generating opportunities for local black women.

Durban African Art Centre
    PO Box 803
    Durban
    4000
    REPUBLIC OF SOUTH AFRICA
    031-3047915

Indwe Sewing Centre
    PO Box 86
    Indwe
    5445
    REPUBLIC OF SOUTH AFRICA
    045522-161

KwaZamokuhle Centre
    PO Box 108
    Estcourt
    3310
    REPUBLIC OF SOUTH AFRICA
    0363-24752

Mdukutshani Beads
    PO Box 6
    Highflats
    4640
    REPUBLIC OF SOUTH AFRICA
    033622-1311

Operation Hunger
    PO Box 32257
    Braamfontein
    2017
    REPUBLIC OF SOUTH AFRICA
    011-4036750

Pondo People
    PO Box
    Port St Johns
    TRANSKEI
    0475-441274

AUTHORS' ACKNOWLEDGMENTS

Many individuals and several organizations have contributed to the compilation of this volume. First, the beadmakers themselves and the many people in KwaZulu and Natal who use and enjoy wearing and displaying beadwork. We hope that they will approve of this book and will take it as a tribute to the art of beadworking in the region. We are indebted, secondly, to Geraldine Morcom for the chapter she contributed to the volume based on her research with the members of the Nazareth Baptist Church. Our thanks are due, thirdly, to the University of Natal for permission to photograph beadwork in the Campbell Collections and the Centre for Oral Studies at the Killie Campbell Africana Library in Durban. In this connection we owe an enormous debt of gratitude to Yvonne Winters, Jenny Harkness and Bobby Eldridge for their help in the selection and identification of suitable items for the volume. The many hours they spent in the preparation of items for photography and in the checking of the text are greatly appreciated. We are also grateful to the African Art Centre in Durban for allowing us to photograph items from their collection and some of those for sale. In particular we would like to acknowledge the assistance of Jo Thorpe, Hlengi Dube, Nomthi Qumza and Lee du Plessis who encouraged us by their interest in the project. Finally our thanks to Herman Oosthuizen and Riva Tustin of the Social Anthropology Department at the University of Natal whose enthusiasm helped to carry us through the long process of research and later the finalization of the text before publication.

Jean Morris
Eleanor Preston-Whyte

ILLUSTRATION ACKNOWLEDGMENTS

African Art Centre Collection, Durban: p. 33 (top); p. 44 (bottom); p. 45; p. 46-7 (top); p. 55 (top); p. 76 (top and bottom); p. 86 (left)

Campbell Collections, Killie Campbell Africana Library, Durban: p. 8 (MM 760); p. 10 (no number); p. 11 (MM 781); p. 12 (top to bottom, MM 1219, MM 2184, MM 1266); p. 13 (MM 1263); p. 14 (MM 1289); p. 15 (top to bottom, MM 1836, MM 1332, MM 769); p. 17; p. 18 (beadwork, top to bottom, MM 1296, MM 1232, MM 1263, MM 1267); p. 25 (top, MM 4159a); pp. 26-7 (MM 2457); p. 30 (cap, MM 4214, waistcoat MM 4245); p. 33 (MM 4251); p. 36 (top, BO 2093, formerly in the African Art Centre Collection); p. 44 (MM 1911); p. 46 (bottom, MM 4122); p. 47 (bottom, MM 4227); p. 48 (top to bottom, MM 3444, MM 2806, MM 3352); p. 50 (top to bottom, MM 4965, MM 4066, MM 4067); p. 51 (top to bottom, MM 2848, MM 2851, MM 4069); pp. 52-3 (top, MM 4246a; bottom, MM 4246b); p. 54 (bottom, MM 3243); p. 55 (left, MM 3282); pp. 56-7 (left to right, MM 2059, MM 2083, MM 2057, MM 2077, MM 2048); p. 58 (MM 2505); p. 59 (top to bottom, MM 4006, MM 3981, MM 3598, MM 3321); p. 71 (right, MM 2771); p. 75 (right, MM 4065); p. 83 (top, MM 2282; bottom, MM 3155)

Preston-Whyte Collection: p. 45; p. 87 (left)

South African Museum, Cape Town: p. 86 (centre, SAM-AE-13416)